T0361221

THE ECONOMICS OF THE
PATENT SYSTEM

FUNDAMENTALS OF PURE AND APPLIED ECONOMICS

EDITORS IN CHIEF

J. LESOURNE, Conservatoire National des Arts et Métiers, Paris, France
H. SONNENSCHEIN, University of Pennsylvania, Philadelphia, PA, USA

ADVISORY BOARD

K. ARROW, Stanford, CA, USA
W. BAUMOL, Princeton, NJ, USA
W. A. LEWIS, Princeton, NJ, USA
S. TSURU, Tokyo, Japan

ECONOMICS OF TECHNOLOGICAL CHANGE I
In 3 Volumes

THE ECONOMICS OF THE PATENT SYSTEM

ERICH KAUFER

First published in 1989 by
Harwood Academic Publishers GmbH

Reprinted in 2001 by
Routledge
2 Park Square, Milton Park, Abingdon, Oxon, OX14 4RN

Transferred to Digital Printing 2007

Routledge is an imprint of the Taylor & Francis Group

© 1989 Harwood Academic Publishers GmbH

All rights reserved. No part of this book may be reprinted or reproduced
or utilized in any form or by any electronic, mechanical,
or other means, now known or hereafter invented, including photocopying
and recording, or in any information storage or retrieval system, without
permission in writing from the publishers.

The publishers have made every effort to contact authors/copyright holders
of the works reprinted in *Harwood Fundamentals of Pure & Applied Economics*.
This has not been possible in every case, however, and we would welcome
correspondence from those individuals/companies we have been unable to
trace.

These reprints are taken from original copies of each book. in many cases
the condition of these originals is not perfect. the publisher has gone to
great lengths to ensure the quality of these reprints, but wishes to point
out that certain characteristics of the original copies will, of necessity, be
apparent in reprints thereof.

British Library Cataloguing in Publication Data
A CIP catalogue record for this book
is available from the British Library

The Economics of the Patent System
ISBN 0-415-26930-X
Economics of Technological Change I: 3 Volumes
ISBN 0-415-26928-8
Harwood Fundamentals of Pure & Applied Economics
ISBN 0-415-26907-5

The Economics of the Patent System

Erich Kaufer
University of Innsbruck, Austria

A volume in the Economics of Technological
Change section

edited by

F. M. Scherer
Swarthmore College, USA

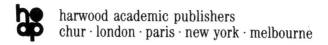
harwood academic publishers
chur · london · paris · new york · melbourne

© 1989 by Harwood Academic Publishers GmbH
Poststrasse 22, 7000 Chur, Switzerland
All rights reserved

Harwood Academic Publishers

Post Office Box 197
London WC2E 9PX
England

58, rue Lhomond
75005 Paris
France

Post Office Box 786
Cooper Station
New York, NY 10276
United States of America

Private Bag 8
Camberwell, Victoria 3124
Australia

Library of Congress Cataloging-in-Publication Data

Kaufer, Erich.
  The economics of the patent system/Erich Kaufer.
  p. cm.—(Fundamentals of pure and applied economics; v. 30.
  Economics of technological change section)
  Bibliography: p.
  Includes index.
  ISBN 3-7186-4870-9
  1. Patents—History.   2. Patents—Economic aspects—History.
  I. Title.   II. Series: Fundamentals of pure and applied economics;
v. 30.   III. Series: Fundamentals of pure and applied economics.
Economics of technological change section.
T215.K38   1988
338.4'36087—dc 19

No part of this book may be reproduced or utilized in any form or
by any means, electronic or mechanical, including photocopying and
recording, or by any information storage or retrieval system, without
permission in writing from the publisher.

Contents

Introduction to the Series

Drawing on a personal network, an economist can still relatively easily stay well informed in the narrow field in which he works, but to keep up with the development of economics as a whole is a much more formidable challenge. Economists are confronted with difficulties associated with the rapid development of their discipline. There is a risk of "balkanization" in economics, which may not be favorable to its development.

Fundamentals of Pure and Applied Economics has been created to meet this problem. The discipline of economics has been subdivided into sections (listed inside). These sections include short books, each surveying the state of the art in a given area.

Each book starts with the basic elements and goes as far as the most advanced results. Each should be useful to professors needing material for lectures, to graduate students looking for a global view of a particular subject, to professional economists wishing to keep up with the development of their science, and to researchers seeking convenient information on questions that incidentally appear in their work.

Each book is thus a presentation of the state of the art in a particular field rather than a step-by-step analysis of the development of the literature. Each is a high-level presentation but accessible to anyone with a solid background in economics, whether engaged in business, government, international organizations, teaching, or research in related fields.

Three aspects of *Fundamentals of Pure and Applied Economics* should be emphasized:

—First, the project covers the whole field of economics, not only theoretical or mathematical economics.

—Second, the project is open-ended and the number of books is not predetermined. If new interesting areas appear, they will generate additional books.

—Last, all the books making up each section will later be grouped to constitute one or several volumes of an Encyclopedia of Economics.

The editors of the sections are outstanding economists who have selected as authors for the series some of the finest specialists in the world.

J. Lesourne   *H. Sonnenschein*

The Economics of the Patent System

ERICH KAUFER*

University of Innsbruck, Austria

1. THE PATENT SYSTEM IN HISTORICAL PERSPECTIVE

In medieval Europe, royal letters closed by a seal were called "litterae clausae;" those that were sealed but open were "litterae patentes." Litterae patentes thus were open documents granting their holder certain rights, privileges, titles, or offices. From this came the nomenclature for modern invention patents, called "letters patent" or simply "patents" in English usage. Litterae patentes were also called "litterae breves," from which the French term "brevets d'invention" evolved. See [94].

1.1. Patents of invention: From discretionary privileges to formal statutes

In Egypt and other ancient cultures, no patent-like institutions have been discovered, and it is likely that none existed, since scientific and technological knowledge was closely held within priestal castes and guarded through secrecy. Patents were also unknown in Greece and the Roman empire, where manual labor was carried out largely by slaves and was not deemed worthy of educated men. Consequently, those who, through their education, were the most likely source of technological progress had little or no interest in it.

Marking the transition from one historical epoch to another is necessarily arbitrary. However, the year 529 A.D. has good claim to being the start of the Middle Ages. For one, in that year the Emperor Justinian closed Plato's Academy at Athens, called by Hegel "the establishment of pagan philosophy." At the same time,

---

* I am deeply indebted to F. M. Scherer, who greatly improved the text both in substance and style. However, all remaining errors are mine.

St. Benedict founded at Monte Cassino a new monastery whose rule, "ora et labora," viewed manual labor as cooperation with God in the task of creation. The departure from antiquity's contempt of manual labor is shown inter alia in Hugo of St. Victor's new (1130 A.D.) systematic view of science. To the tripartite ancient classification of sciences into "logic," "theory," and "ethics," Hugo added the "artes mechanicae," whose practice was a divinely-ordained foil against infirmities of the human body.

In the Middle Ages, the pace of technological change accelerated dramatically. See [31, pp. 158–181]. Italian cities like Florence, Lucca, Milan, and Venice became leaders in artisan production. However, secrecy, often enforced in the Italian city-states by draconian penalties, was used to protect technological advantages and avoid the disclosure of important know-how. See [155, pp. 28–29]. This propensity changed with the emergence of a patent system.

In tandem came changes in the way the process of "invention" was perceived. The practice of granting property rights in what we now call inventions had its historical roots in mining law [98, 121, 155]. During the Middle Ages, the term "invention" had a meaning much closer to what we would now call "discovery," e.g., of new ore resources, than the meaning accepted under modern patent law. In medieval Latin, "invenire" meant (accidental) discovery, while "ars" was used to connote derived technological know-how. Medieval orders in the archives of Innsbruck, Austria, consistently refer to "Perkwerks Erfyndung," that is, to the "invention" of mining sites.

The Alps were an ore mining area from at least the time of the Celtic settlement. In such mining areas, there was a long common law tradtion concerning the mining, timber use, and water use property rights of those who were first to "invent" an ore site. As new ore locations were found in Saxony, Silesia, and Bohemia, the miners brought their unwritten common law with them. The law then became incorporated into the decisions of specialized mining courts and into the "Constitutiones Juris Metallici" promulgated by King Wenceslaus II in the year 1300 [184].

When surface ore deposits were exhausted and mining efforts had to go deeper, it became increasingly difficult to draw ground water from the mines. Around the year 1500, for example, the Fugger silver mines in Tyrol employed up to 600 people carrying water up ladders in buckets. One of the earliest alternatives to this labor-intensive approach was to dig water draining galleries. Those who financed the digging were protected by special privileges allowing them to receive a designated share of the mined ore and preventing rivals from digging competing galleries "sine stollonarii licentia speciali" (without a special license) from the gallery owner [184, p. 148]. Accompanying these rights was the obligation to maintain and extend the galleries in tandem with the progress of ore mining.

Similar privileges were then extended to those who devised so-called "Wasserkuenste" (literally, "water arts"), that is, mechanical means for drawing the water from the mines. The law concerning the "first to invent an ore site" was applied directly to the first person to invent a mechanical draining device. Usually, the inventor received a fixed reward after he had put his idea into practice. If the device was expensive, the inventor was paid an advance sum to finance the construction. It was also common to complement the fixed reward with a time-limited claim on some share of the mine's output. Others were prevented from imitating the draining technology "sine . . . licentia speciali."

During the 14th and 15th centuries, the Republic of Venice attracted numerous persons skilled in building "Wasserkuenste" for mines. Water mill capacity had to be expanded, water had to be pumped from the lagunes, and the canals had to be dredged. Venice also sought to develop ore mining on the Italian "Terra Ferma" it had conquered. Northerners meeting these demands characteristically requested special privileges protecting them against established local competition. In 1323, the first known privilege was asked by a master milling engineer Joannes Teuthonicus from Germany, who promised to build so many grain mills that the whole demand of Venice could be satisfied. He was promised a sum of up to 80 ducats for the construction of a model mill and a "just compensation," to be determined by the judgement of two experts, if his mill proved to be useful. Thus, the Venetian administration did not issue a privilege for the mere discovery of a new mechanical idea. Rather, it insisted that a model be built which would serve as a basis for judging whether the idea would work and be useful. It is uncertain whether Joannes actually received the grant, but in the following decades, a number of grain mill construction privileges were in fact granted. In addition to fixed fees for the construction of mills, the Venetian government promised the privilege holders a specified minimum amount of work orders at a fixed price for a limited period of time.

In 1409, Venice granted the German Henricus von Heslingen a privilege to exploit an ore mine and use needed water and timber according to the common law prevailing in Germany. In the following decades, Venetian ore mining grew rapidly, necessitating a more formalized legal status. In 1488 the Venetian Senate promulgated the *Statuto Mineraria*. A German language copy— evidently for use by German miners in the service of the Republic— exists in the archives of Innsbruck [83]. Careful inspection reveals it to be in large measure a copy of the *Schladminger Bergbrief*—a Tyrolean mining order from the year 1408 [82].

Meanwhile, institutions were also evolving to deal with "inventions"—often called "edificium et ingenium" in the Latin texts—of a more specifically technological character. They took two rather different forms. One important example was the privilege granted by the Venetian Senate in 1460 to a young German, Jacobus de Valperga, who had devised a new type of water pump. The grant stated that as long as Jacobus lived, no one could make the pump without an express license from Jacobus. Violation carried a penalty of 1,000 ducats and destruction of the offending machinery. However, Jacobus was obliged to grant licenses if reasonable royalties were offered. Thus, the focus was on preventing imitation of Jacobus' machine *without his permission,* and the privilege was limited by what we would now call a compulsory licensing provision. In contrast, another privilege granted in the same year to master engineer Guilielmus Lombardus reserved to Guilielmus exclusive monopoly rights in making certain furnaces, with no provision for "compulsory" licensing. The Venetian administrative practice distinguished between an invention privilege and a trade privilege. Jacobus asked for protection guaranteeing him license revenues from all who used his invention. Guilielmus, on the other hand, received a guarantee that no one could compete with him in selling the product that incorporated his invention.

Monopoly privileges, with or without licensing provisions, were not the only way Venice sought to foster technical advance. Venice's large and important naval weapons factory, the Arsenale, is not known to have conferred them. As the precursor of today's nationalized enterprise, the Arsenale instead attracted technically skilled persons by offering high salaries and benefits such as free housing.

As the 15th century progressed, Venice experienced a period of severe financial difficulties, partly because of its wars to extend its claims on the Italian Terra Ferma and partly because of threats from the Turks. It therefore placed increasing emphasis on monopoly privileges as a substitute for government subsidies. In 1474, only a year after the Senate decided to build the Arsenale Novissimo, a formal patent code was promulgated. Its preamble states:

We have among us men of great genius, apt to invent and discover igenious devices . . . . Now, if provisions were made for the works and devices discovered by such persons, so that others who may see them could not build them and take the inventor's honor away, more men would then apply their genius, would discover, and would build devices of great utility to our commonwealth [52, p. 11].[1]

The code specified that the subject invention had to be proven workable and useful, if only by means of a model. This requirement dated back at least to the case of Joannes Teuthonicus. Also, no

---

[1] In his translation, Gilfillan says "apt to invent and discover . . . ," where the Venetian text uses the words "apti ad excogitar et trovar." Recall that the Latin "invenire" was used in the sense, "to discover accidentally," i.e., trovar, whereas "excogitar" is more properly translated as "to devise," that is, to invent in today's sense of the word.

It may be useful to have the relevant text in its original, drawn from [97, p. 518]:

El sono in questa Città, et anche ala zornada, per la grandeza et bontà soa concorre homeni da diverse bande, et accutissimi ingegni, apti ad excogitar et trovar varij ingegnosi artificij. Et sel fosse provisto, che le opere et artificij trovado da loro, altri viste che le havesseno, non podesseno farle, et tuor honor suo, simel homeni exercitariano l'ingegno, troveriano et fariano dele chosse, che sariano de non picola utilità et beneficio al stado nostro.

L'andara parte che per auctorità de questo Conseio, chadaun che farà in questa Città algun nuovo et ingegnoso artificio, non facto per avanti nel dominio nostro, reducto chel sara a perfection, siche el se possi usar, et exercitar, sia tegnudo darlo in nota al officio di nostri provededori de Commun. Siando prohibito a chadaun altro in alguna terra e luogo nostro, far algun altro artificio, ad imagine et similitudine de quello, senza consentimento et licentia del auctor, fino ad anni X. Et tamen se algun el fesse, lo auctor et inventor predicto, habia libertà poderlo citar a chadaun officio de questa Città, dal qual officio, el dicto, che havesse contrafacto, sia astreto a pagarli ducati centro, et l'artificio subito sia disfacto. Siando però in libertà de la nostra Signoria, ad ogni suo piaxer, tuor et usar ne i suo bisogni chadaun di dicti artificij, et instrumenti, cum questa però condition, che altri cha i auctori non li possi exercitar.

imitation was permitted for ten years without express permission from the inventor. However, the Republic retained the right to use the invention for its own purposes. An otherwise unauthorized use carried a penalty of one hundred ducats and destruction of the offending device. But the administrative practice that followed also included provisions for compulsory licensing and the revocation of patents not used commercially. Thus, the patent code, based in large part upon the decision in the matter of Jacobus de Valperga, must be seem as an instrument designed to attract engineers to the Republic. It was not an instrument to stimulate artisan production by granting monopolistic trade privileges.

The 1474 patent code saw little direct use. From 1474 through 1490, only three patents were issued, and one of them referred to the Senate's 1474 decree, probably because it conferred substantial monopoly privileges in using public water. But those privileges served as models for later privilege applications. Over the period 1490–1550, covered in a penetrating study by Mandich [97], 120 privileges were granted, most involving water mills, wind mills, pumps, dredging machines, and similar mechanical devices. These privileges did not refer expressly to the 1474 code, but followed similar principles. Some resembled in spirit the grant to Jacobus de Valperga. But even in those cases, the patent's duration was not a fixed term of ten years, but varied between 5 and 80 years. Other privileges were monopolistic trade privileges like the one issued to Guilielmus Lombardus.

As the grant of patents spread northward, and with the emergence of absolutist governments, tension mounted between grants with licensing provisions and those that conferred unconditional monopoly privileges, with or without some element of invention or innovation. Under the reign of Queen Elizabeth I in England, patent grants were used increasingly to implement mercantilist policy, and especially to benefit royal favorites. Parliament and the Crown clashed over who had, or ought to have, the prerogative of granting monopoly privileges. In 1623, Parliament prevailed decisively, passing the *Statute of Monopolies*. See [85]. Among other privileges, patents were declared to be illegal, except for grants to the true and first inventor or inventors of a new manufacture. Newness had no international meaning; it was sufficient if the manufacture was new to England. The duration of such a patent was to be fourteen years. This term was chosen because it encompassed the time it took to train two successive generations of apprentices, each serving a term of seven years. Thus, Parliament expressed its desire to protect the know-how accumulated by masters in implementing an invention.

In France, systematic use of patents as an instrument of mercantilist policy began in the middle of the 16th century. See [155, pp. 209–252]. For the most part, privileges were granted only after a careful review of the benefits from encouraging a new trade. The monopoly restrictions were usually limited to a geographic boundary (une banlieue) of ten miles (lieues), but narrower (2 lieues) or wider (50 lieues) territorial boundaries were sometimes set. In the first decades of the 18th century, such restrictions came increasingly to be used to protect established trades and manufacturers. Even before the Revolution, public opinion gravitated toward rejecting patents as contrary to the freedom of trade. To underline the break with the past brought about by the Revolution, the patent law of 1791 spoke only of "brevets d'inventions" and declared that the inventor had a natural property right to his invention. In this, the previous view of patents as a grant of royal privilege was replaced by a justification rooted in the rights of the citizen.

In the "Constituante" debate over French patent law, the British patent system, as it had evolved from the Statute of Monopolies, was referred to as a model case. It also became a model for British colonies in North America. Massachusetts passed a similar law in 1641. Connecticut followed suit in 1672. South Carolina (1691) was the first to speak of patents not as sovereign grants, but as a fulfillment of the rights of the inventor.

More than one hundred years passed before there were significant new developments. Then, in 1782, the American Constitution gave Congress the power:

... to promote the progress of science and useful arts, by securing for limited times to authors and inventors the exclusive right to their respective writings and discoveries.

In 1790 the first U.S. federal patent law was promulgated. Like its predecessor in South Carolina, it rested in the premise that the inventor had a right to claim a patent on what he had invented.

Furthermore, in order to ensure that patents were granted only for "new and useful" inventions, an official examination prior to the patent's issuance was required. In 1793, this prior examination was replaced by mere notification to the Secretary of State (initially, Thomas Jefferson). But in 1836, it was reinstituted, and it has been a part of the U.S. patent system, like most modern patent systems, ever since. See [94, 114, 175].

1.2. The Antipatent Movement: Near Success and Sudden Defeat

In the German-speaking parts of Europe, monopoly privileges had a varied history. See [155, pp. 252–289]. Empress Maria Theresia of Austria was unsympathetic, refusing to grant privileges because she found them "hoechst schaedlich" (highly detrimental). See [129, p. 153]. Her adversary, Frederik of Prussia, adopted a more receptive policy, granting numerous monopoly privileges for the introduction of new arts. Yet in Austria as in Prussia, monopoly privileges had been established in many trades as the nineteenth century dawned. There, as in the western European lands, they were widely disliked as misuses of royal prerogative.

This association between patents and monopoly privileges gave birth to an energetic anti-patent movement [94]. The seeds were sown by the Napoleonic reordering of the German territories. Some territories in the Rhine area adopted the French patent law of 1791. The territories of southern Germany gave up the practice of privileged grants. But soon "polytechnical associations" were founded, lobbying for the introduction of patent laws and, especially in Bavaria and Wuerttemberg, for tariff protection. By 1825, both kingdoms had laws granting patents on inventions that were new to the kingdom.

Tension rose as Prussia began to dominate policy among the German territories. In 1806, after its defeat by Napolean, Prussia instituted reforms under which a new kind of civil servant, nourished inter alia on the ideas of Adam Smith, gained power. The Prussian government pushed for free trade among the German territories, and as remnants of mercantilist policy, patents were seen as a barrier to free trade. By 1862, all tariffs had been abolished inside Germany. In that same year, a free trade treaty with France marked the high point of the free trade movement's influence. The Prussian government argued concurrently that all patent laws in the German territories should be abolished [155, pp. 271–281].

A similarly strong anti-patent movement led to the repeal of the Dutch patent law in 1869. In 1872, the British House of Lords accepted a substantial revision of existing patent law. Between 1849 and 1863, the Swiss parliament rejected four petitions to introduce a patent law [94].

However, strong counter-forces were also in motion. Prussia was an agrarian state at the beginning of the 19th century. Between 1850 and 1870, the German territories, especially the Prussian ones, were industrializing rapidly. Industrial leaders like the Siemens brothers, one working in Berlin and the other in London, organized pro-patent support groups. Second, world exhibitions emerged, and participation in them became a matter of national prestige. Germany received its first genuine recognition as an industrial nation at the Paris exhibition of 1867. Potential American participants refused to participate in the Vienna exhibition of 1873 unless the German nations agreed to provide provisional patent protection on the American inventions put on display. Third, the free trade movement in Prussia proved to have shallow roots. Since Austria under the Habsburg monarchy had adopted a strongly protectionist development policy, the creation of a German free trade area was a political tactic used by Prussia for excluding Austria from the German union. Once this goal was achieved, the free trade movement was supported less vigorously. Fourth, at the 1873 Vienna exhibition, a patent congress proposed to introduce into national patent laws strict compulsory licensing principles. To the extent that the proposal was accepted, it undermined the objection that patents were mere mercantilist monopoly privileges. Fifth and finally, the year 1873 marked the onset of a worldwide depression, which in turn precipitated a movement away from free trade and toward protectionism. Tariffs and patents now appeared to be important protectionist instruments.

With these changes, the anti-patent tide ebbed. In 1874, the British government backed off from the drastic patent reform proposal already approved by the House of Lords. In 1877, the German Reich adopted a patent law.

Switzerland played a wavering but pivotal role in the new patent law developments. Patent laws were rejected by popular referenda in Switzerland in 1866 and 1882. Nevertheless, Switzerland participated actively in drafting the Paris Convention, signed in 1883 by Belgium, Brazil, France, Guatemala, Italy, the Netherlands, Por-

tugal, Spain, El Salvador, and Serbia as well as Switzerland. The
Convention created mechanisms for world-wide patent grant coor-
dination. Although it had no patent system of its own, Switzerland
was charged with administering and supervising the Paris Convention. In accepting this role, the Swiss government agreed to initiate
a domestic patent system as soon as possible. Meanwhile, Swiss
public opinion was changing, in part because one of the largest
Swiss industries, the watch industry, was experiencing intense
competition from imitators. In July 1887, a Swiss patent statute was
overwhelmingly approved in a referendum. However, because the
newly emerging Swiss chemical industry still found it advantageous
to imitate the technology of its more advanced German rivals, the
Swiss law limited patentability to mechanical inventions only. This
prompted the German Reich to threaten Switzerland with retalia-
tory tariffs. In 1907 Switzerland backed off, extending coverage
under its patent law to chemical process inventions (but not product
inventions) [17, 73, 91].

2. AN OVERVIEW OF THE PATENT SYSTEM's OPERATION

2.1. Similarities and differences in national patent systems

The law of the United States declares that a patent can be issued
for "any new and useful process, machine, manufacture, or
composition of matter, or any new and useful improvement
thereof."[2] "New" and "useful" are key words, subject to much
debate and evolution over time. Before a patent is issued, the
application is examined in the U.S. to ensure that the necessary
standards of patentability are maintained. Similar approaches are
followed in other Western nations.[3] However, there are numerous
differences in detail among the various national systems.

---

[2] 35 U.S. Code 101, as amended in 1952.
[3] This review largely ignores the Soviet and Eastern European patent systems,
which for a full exposition would require a more extended analysis than is possible
here. Among other things, there are differences rooted in ideology. Under
capitalism, the patent is a private property right that permits the functioning of a
market for inventions and their use. Under socialist doctrine, an inventor is entitled
to an inventor's certificate whose function is to provide a reward to the extent that
his invention has been useful to society. Ideology apart, one might say that the
Soviet patent system is a system of public prizes for inventions, whereas the capitalist
patent is a system of private property rights. See [8, 40] for more information on
patent systems in socialist nations.

One important difference concerns the determination of who the first inventor is when conflicts arise. Under American law, the patent is awarded to the first person to invent, which in turn requires a complex weighing of priority in having the original insight, disclosing it through a patent application, and reducing the invention to practice. Most other nations follow the continental European approach, granting the patent to the first who files an application for a patent on a specific invention.

Determining whether an invention is genuinely inventive and useful is equally problematic. Section 103 or the U.S. Patent Act, as amended in 1952, provides that "A patent may not be obtained . . . if the . . . subject matter as a whole would not have been obvious at the time the invention was made to a person having ordinary skill in the art." Apparently rejecting earlier court interpretations that required inventions to reveal "the flash of creative genius" and not merely result from trial and error, the 1952 Patent Act states that "patentability shall not be negated by the manner in which the invention was made" [74].

Inventions must also be shown to be useful. However, under U.S. law in doubtful cases, the benefit of the doubt is usually resolved in favor of the application, since only later development may provide conclusive proof of utility.[4]

To let the issuing authorities apply these tests and also to make known to the public what has been invented, patent applicants are required to describe their inventions to such an extent that an average expert in the field can implement the invention on the basis of what is revealed in the patent document. However, this disclosure requirement is difficult to enforce, just as it is hard to tell whether an invention is really new and useful. A large patent office like that of West Germany had a stock of 27.5 million patent documents in 1985, to which some half million documents per year relating to roughly 300,000 new inventions in various parts of the world are added each year. Processing large numbers of patent applications and accommodating the huge worldwide patent literature requires compromises in the stringency with which the standards of patentability are enforced. Large patent offices employ

---

[4] See the U.S. Court of Customs Appeals decision *in re Hofstetter*, 15 U.S.P.Q. 105, 109 (1966).

hundreds of degree-holding scientists and engineers and thousands of supporting personnel. They take roughly two years on average to process a typical patent application.[5] Yet no matter how much care is taken, perfectly consistent and accurate decisions are not possible.

In many nations, rights falling short of those conferred by a full-fledged invention patent may also be obtained. For example, under German law, the inventor can apply for a so-called *Gebrauchsmuster*, or "petty patent" [36]. The Gebrauchsmuster, valid for three years and renewable for a second three years, is obtainable only for inventions resulting in a special, unchangeable product form. Because the Gebrauchsmuster is issued speedily, inventors tend to file for patents and Gebrauchsmuster simultaneously. Nearly one West German patent application in every two is accompanied by a Gebrauchsmuster registration.[6] Similar petty patents play an important role in Japan. They are found also in Brazil, Italy, the Philippines, Portugal, Spain, South Korea, and Venezuela.

Under the European Patent Convention, the life of Europe-wide and member nation patents is 20 years, beginning with the date of application. United States patents have a life of 17 years in most cases, but the clock is not started until the patent is actually issued. Less developed and newly industrializing nations tend to allow shorter patent lives.

There are important differences among nations in the subject matter that can be patented. The U.S., Japanese, European, and South African patent laws grant patents on both product and process inventions without discriminating among fields of use. In Switzerland, as noted earlier, and also in other nations, there had been a long-standing policy of granting patents on chemical

---

[5] Scherer [148, p. 108; and 149, p. 20] reports an average lag of 19 months for the United States during the early 1970s and a lag of up to six years for Japan. From a private communication with the German Patent Office, the average lag was 2.7 years in 1986.

[6] A 1987 revision of the Gebrauchsmuster law extends the coverage to electrical (and other, e.g., hydraulic) circuits embodied in a product. It also permitted extensions in a third term of two years, thus permitting a total life of eight years. Gebrauchsmuster applications can be filed after a patent application has been made, in which case the patent application date becomes the effective date for the Gebrauchsmuster. [181]

processes but not on chemical substances. Italy systematically excluded drugs from patent protection until 1978, when its Constitutional Court ruled the exemption to be unconstitutional. India's policy typifies that of the less developed nations. Whereas the normal patent life is 14 years, patents on foodstuffs, pharmaceuticals, and agro-chemical products are limited to seven years, and after three years, the patent holder is required to grant licenses to other would-be users.

Not all patents stay in force through their maximum legally permissible lives. Many nations, including West Germany, Austria, France, Great Britain, the Netherlands, Japan, Switzerland, and (since October 1982) the United States, require periodic renewal fees to be paid to maintain the patent owner's rights. West Germany and Austria in particular have traditionally enforced schedules under which the renewal fees escalate sharply as time passes. In Germany during 1986, for example, renewal fees during the first ten years of a patent's life cumulated to a total of DM 2,375. However, by the end of the 20th year, a patent holder must have paid a total of DM 22,375 to keep its patent in force. A consequence of rising renewal fees is the weeding out of marginal patents—those whose value is less than the marginal cost of the fee. Taylor and Silberston [164, p. 97] report that after nine years, roughly 50 percent of initially issued British patents were still in force, and only about 18 percent of the patents remained in force throughout the maximum term allowed by law. In Germany, with a more steeply rising fee schedule, the rate over time has been even higher. Studies of experience prior to World War II revealed that only 2.5 to 5 percent of all initially issued patents survived to their terminal year [111]. However, there is reason to believe that the fraction of survivors has increased more recently.[7]

Especially when international trade is vigorous, the geographic area over which patent holders compete is often wider than the area within which national patent protection exists. Prussia's efforts to create a German customs union with homogeneous patent policies were an early example of the effort to reconcile such disparities. On a broader international plane, the Paris Patent Convention was the

---

[7] Deutsches Patentamt, *Blatt fuer Patent-, Muster-, und Zeichenwesen,* vol. 77 (1975), p. 82, and vol. 89 (1987), p. 94.

first attempt to integrate national patent territories with the area of effective competition. It provides that a foreign patent application is treated in the same manner as a domestic applicant. A key Paris Convention element is the principle of union priority, according to which a priority claim established in one member country shall be recognized in all other member countries. Thus, an inventor who has filed a valid patent application in his home nation may wait for up to twelve months before filing an application in other member nations without losing the priority right to his invention. In 1987, the Paris Patent Convention had been adopted by 97 member states, including 30 industrialized western nations, 12 eastern (i.e., Communist) nations, and 55 less-developed nations.

An International Patent Cooperation Treaty signed in 1970 and effective in June 1978 simplified the procedures for acquiring patent protection internationally. Under it, an inventor can select a group of up to 40 participating nations (in 1987) for which he wishes to have patent protection. He files an application in a single official language for those nations at one of four major patent offices—in Europe, Japan, the United States, or the Soviet Union—conducting international patentability searches. Eighteen months after the date of filing, the application is published by the World Intellectual Property Organization in Geneva. Up to 20 months after the international search report has been issued by the patent office in which the application was filed, the applicant has to submit the report to the various national patent offices in order to obtain national patents. From that point on, application becomes a national procedure. At the end of 1986, 42,583 patent applications had been registered under these international rules.

Within Europe, further progress toward internationalization of patenting procedures has been made. On June 1, 1978, the European Patent Convention became effective. As of 1986, 13 nations—Austria, Belgium, France, Germany, Great Britain, Greece, Holland, Italy, Liechtenstein, Luxembourg, Spain, Sweden, and Switzerland—had joined. Under it, national patent laws have been adjusted to a European standard. To obtain a so-called Europatent, an inventor files an application to the European Patent Office in Munich, to its branches in the Hague or West Berlin, or to his national patent office. Within three months he or she has to provide a translation into either English, French, or German. The fee charged depends upon the number of nations for which the inventor seeks patent protection. Calculations by Greif [57] show that the applicant for a Europatent intended to be valid to three nations pays lower filing fees on average than it would filing three separate applications in each nation. To keep a Europatent in force, renewal fees analogous to those charged under the separate national systems must be paid. Greif's calculations suggest that when these renewal fees and also the cost of routine patent infringement monitoring are taken into account along with filing costs, a Europatent valid in three nations is less expensive on average than patents obtained separately in two national jurisdictions.

Patents issued by the European Patent Office are still only a bundle of national patent rights, enforceable according to local law in the individual national jurisdictions. A convention to create a truly European patent was signed on December 15, 1975. It calls for a single European Community patent to be valid in all member states of the Community, replacing the rights under separate national patents. However, because the convention had not been ratified by the parliaments of all EC nations, it had not yet become effective by 1987, when this was written.

2.2. Changes in the inventive process and patenting trends

In principle, patents are granted to the individual or individuals who invent some new product or process. This approach can be traced back to the fact that when patent systems first emerged, nearly all inventive activity was carried out by individual inventors working more or less alone, without formal organizational attachments. But over the years, radical changes have occurred in the nature of inventive activity. Three changes are of particular importance. First, although remnants of the past remain, invention has come to depend more and more closely upon a base of advancing knowledge. This is a relatively new development; as former Harvard president James B. Conant observed [32, p. 58], " ... for an amazingly long time advances in science and progress in the practical arts ran parallel with few interconnecting ties." Indeed, according to Alfred North Whitehead [179, p. 126], the greatest invention of the 19th century was the invention of the method of how to invent. That method—the systematic exploration of invention possibilities by persons trained in modern science and engineering—came to fruition with the emergence of modern research and development laboratories. The German chemical companies, Robert Fulton's work on steam-propelled boats, Thomas Edison's Menlo Park laboratory (eventually a part of the General Electric Co.) and Alexander Graham Bell's laboratory in Boston (the forerunner of Bell Telephone Laboratories) were pioneers during the last few decades of the 19th century [96]. Thus, a second major institutional change was the movement of inventive activity from the realm of the independent, individual inventor to form corporate organizations. Third, technology and the scope of business firms' operations have become increasingly international-ized. Patents therefore have been used to protect inventions not merely within a city state like Venice or a nation state like 19th Century Germany, but the whole world.

These changes are reflected in statistics on the origin of patents within diverse national patenting jurisdictions. Thus, at the begin-ning of the 20th Century, U.S. corporations received only seven percent of all patents issued in the United States, while 82 percent went to unaffiliated individuals. By the early 1980s, the share of American patents received by individuals had fallen to 18 percent, while the share of domestic corporations rose to 42 percent. Another striking change has been the increasing role of foreign inventors. At the turn of the century, few foreigners bothered to seek American patents. During the 1960s, U.S. corporations obtained 55 percent of American patents while foreign corporations received 13.6 percent. By the early 1980s, the share of foreign corporations had risen to 30 percent.

Compared to other nations, the United States remained relatively self-sufficient in terms of patent originations. Table I provides wider-ranging insight into the extent of international patenting. The first two numerical columns suggest that the number of patents issued within a nation tends to rise with the size and the level of economic development (although other factors such as the strin-gency of patentability requirements also matter). The second set of numerical columns shows the fraction of a given nation's patents that originated from the residents of other nations. Again, the larger the nation and the higher its level of economic development, the smaller is the share of its patents foreigners obtain. The third set

TABLE I
Patents granted in selected groups of nations in 1967 and 1980.

	Number of patents granted in		Share of patents held by foreigners		Patents granted to the country's residents in foreign nations as a percent of patents granted to residents in the home country	
	1967	1980	1967	1980	1967	1980
	Group A: Selected industrialized nations					
Belgium	16,627	5,918	90.5%	85.9%	170.3%	205.5%
France	46,995	28,055	67.6	69.9	94.4	148.4
Holland	2,235	3,224	85.6	87.4	2261.8	1430.2
Italy	35,256	8,000	74.3	77.4	61.9	324.7
Switzerland	21,850	5,961	75.3	75.3	231.1	666.2
U.K.	38,790	23,804	74.7	78.3	179.3	216.0
West Germany	13,426	20,188	62.0	51.3	815.0	343.0
Japan	20,773	46,100	33.2	17.5	49.3	54.3
U.S.A.	71,613	61,827	20	40	144.0	146.3
	Group B: Selected industrializing nations					
Brazil	946	3,843	72.3	90.9	24.0	32.4
S. Korea	359	1,419	42.3	81.8	9.7	19.4
Spain	9,585	9,224	71.2	83.9	22.7	79.5
	Group C: Selected less-developed nations					
African Intellectual Property Organization	574	571	100.0	95.4	0	0
Ecuador	131	110	96.2	93.6	0	0
India	3,771	2,500	88.7	80.0	16.8	11.4

Source: Evenson [42, pp. 102–105].

of two columns shows patents received abroad by a nation's residents as a percentage of patents received at home by that nation's residents. In effect, the data show how aggressively domestic patent holders reach out to achieve foreign patent protection. Here the pattern is less clear. Dutch patent holders obtained in 1980 14 patents abroad for every one gained at home, West Germans 3.4 patents, French 1.5 patents, Americans 1.5, and Brazilians 0.3.

Differences in national patenting in part reflect differences in national patent laws. In Japan, for example, patent applicants were allowed until 1975 to include only one inventive claim per patent, whereas in other countries it was possible to bundle numerous claims—sometimes more than one hundred—into a single patent. Even since 1975, the practice of making only a single claim per patent in Japan has tended to persist, and so an invention involving five claims might be protected by only a single patent in Europe but five patents in Japan.

Within a given national patent jurisdiction, different patent seekers pursue varying policies as to how aggressively they will seek patent protection and where the margin between patenting and not patenting will be drawn in the spectrum over which the quality and scope of particular inventions varies. The most thorough exploration of such differences in "the propensity to patent" has been conducted by Scherer [140, 143, 148]. His newest analysis covers the 1976–77 patenting of 443 U.S. corporations whose activities were disaggregated into 4,274 manufacturing "lines of business." Aggregating the data back up to the level of 22 broad industry groups, he found that the number of patents received per million dollars of 1974 company-financed research and development expenditures ranged from 0.45 (in motor vehicles and other transportation equipment) to 3.98 (in industrial electrical equipment), with a mean for all industry groups of 1.70. Disaggregating to the line of business data and dividing the lines into 250 manufacturing industry categories, he found that the number of patents obtained was strongly influenced both by the amount of R&D expenditure incurred by a line and by the particular industry in which the line operated. Eighty-five percent of the inter-line variance in patenting could be "explained" using these R&D and industry category variables, with roughly half accounted for by differences in R&D spending and the other half by industry-specific differences in the number of patents obtained per million dollars of R&D. The implication is that differences in the propensity to patent are important—indeed, about as important as differences in company research and development spending. A further analysis showed that for a given line of business, the likelihood of receiving at least one patent in a nine-month period rose in a logistic curve-like pattern with the amount spent on R&D by the line. With a yearly R&D budget of $100,000, the probability of receiving a patent was 0.3. As R&D outlays increased to $1 million, the probability of patenting rose to 0.7 and approached certainty (probability = 1.0) with outlays of $10 million.

The propensity to patent appears to differ not only among industries within a given nation, but also over time and across different nation states. Evenson [42] found that the output of patents per scientist and engineer decreased in all U.S. industries over the period from 1964 to 1977. Similar declines over time were observed for Japan, France, the United Kingdom, West Germany, and a larger group of 44 industrialized, semi-industrialized, less-developed, and centrally planned economies.

2.3. Patents as an appropriation mechanism

The original concept of the patent protection was that, by preventing others from imitating an inventor's invention or by putting the inventor in a position to license imitators only in exchange for compensation, patents allow inventors to "appropriate" the economic benefits flowing from their inventive contributions. The expectation of such rewards is what provides an incentive to invent. Absent patent protection, imitation might occur so swiftly that an inventor could appropriate at best a small fraction of his invention's benefits, and if the expected amount were too small, an incentive failure would occur and desirable inventions would not be forthcoming. See [67, 68, 92, 112, 122, and 156].

As inventive activity has moved from the realm of self-standing individual inventors to the corporate research and development laboratory, it has been questioned whether this logic still holds. There are three main problems.

For one, "invention" in the accepted sense is only a part, and sometimes only a small part, of the activity that must be sustained to bring new technology into the marketplace. Substantial research and development expenditures may be incurred in perfecting an invention for commercial exploitation, i.e., "reducing it to practice," and additional sums may have to be invested in plant and equipment and introductory marketing.

This problem is not as new as it might seem. It is found also in the history of James Watt's famous steam engine "invention" [139]. When Watt in 1765, while repairing a model of Newcomen's steam engine, suddenly conceived the idea of a separate condenser to evacuate the cylinder, he had made an invention. Within three days, he had a working model, and thus satisfied the normal requirements for patenting his invention. Yet he needed eleven years and expenditures equivalent to 60 man years of skilled labor before his first perfected steam engine was ready for the marketplace. Without patent protection, it is questionable whether Watt and his financial backers would have invested the funds in carrying out what we would now call the "development" stage of the research and development sequence. Thus, as the British Parliament explicitly recognized in extending the life of Watt's patent to the year 1800, the patent system's objective even in the 18th century may have been to encourage "investment" as much as to stimulate "invention" in a narrow sense.

Second, now as then, patents are far from perfect as a means of appropriating the benefits flowing from an investment in research, invention, and development. Rarely is a patent so strong that it is immune against a determined effort to circumvent it or challenge its validity in the courts. Indeed, the patent system embodies a kind of paradox, for the disclosure of technical details required to obtain a patent often helps would-be imitators in their circumvention efforts. Mansfield and associates [101] found that on average, inventing around a patent requires substantially less cost, and takes less time, than making the original invention.

Third, patents may on the other hand not be *necessary* in appropriating sufficient benefits to motivate investment in research, invention, and development. For one thing, secrecy is an alternative, especially on production processes that will be used in plants closed to visitors and whose employees are bound by non-disclosure contracts. Also, as "invention" has moved from the independent inventor to the corporate laboratory, research and development have become important instruments of corporate competitive strategy, and the strategies pursued may include alternative means of appropriating rewards sufficient to justify the inventive effort. In oligopolistic industries, already existing barriers to entry may protect incumbent firms from rapid imitation after they have made and adopted an invention. At the same time, fear of losing profitable market share, either to rival oligopolists or (when entry through innovation is open) to technologically facile newcomers may spur R&D efforts. Second, product differentiation and "image" advantages may accrue to firms successfully introducing new inventions to the market, especially when the responsible firm is a "first mover." See [20; 33; 53; 147, pp. 445–446; and 151]. Given such advantages, the firm may be able to hold substantial market shares and sell at prices exceeding production costs even without patent protection. Third, the corporation that introduces some new technology first, or at an early date, may aggressively exploit its invention in the maket place, racing down a "learning curve" and gaining a decisive cost advantage over less aggressive rivals [21, 62, 158] Again, this advantage and the profits it sustains may accrue, whether or not the inventor has effective patent protection.

Various empirical studies have attempted to determine how effective and important patent protection is as a means of appropriating the rewards from invention. Among the earlier efforts, Scherer's [137] and one by Taylor and Silberston [164] are the most thorough. They found that the importance of patents varies widely from industry to industry and probably also as a function of firm size, small firms placing more weight on the need for patent protection than large. Patents were viewed as a critical inducement to research and development investment only in a few industries such as pharmaceuticals, speciality chemicals, and some mechanical engineering lines. Their importance in pharmaceuticals stems from the large research, development, and clinical testing expenditures required to introduce a new drug; the ease of imitating a proven drug without repeating those outlays; and the strong protection a patent gives for chemical molecules that have been proven superior to different near-substitute molecules.

Wider-ranging quantitative insights emerge from a new and still incomplete study by Levin and associates [87]. Levin *et al.* administered questionnaires to some 650 research and development executives on the importance of diverse appropriation mechanisms in 130 manufacturing lines of business. The respondents were asked inter alia to evaluate the effectiveness of patents, secrecy, lead time advantages, learning-by-doing advantages, and superior sales or service as means of capturing the benefits from new or improved products and new or improved production processes. Answers were scored on a scale from 1 (for "not at all effective") to 7 (for "very effective"). For product inventions, superior sales and service were ranked as most important on average, followed closely by lead time advantages and learning-by-doing advantages. Patent protection tended to receive much less weight, although there were exceptions in a few industries—notably, pharmaceuticals, agricultural chemicals, and industrial organic chemicals, where patents received scores exceeding 6.0; and synthetic rubber, glass, compressors, and power-driven hand tools, where average scores above 5.0 were nonetheless exceeded by the scores on some other dimension. Superior sales and service received average scores above 5.0 in four-fifths of the industries, while patents were rated that highly in only one-fifth of the industries. For process inventions, patents again trailed lead time, learning-by-doing advantages, secrecy, and sales and service effort in that order as means of capturing benefits. Not surprisingly, patents were considered more effective on average than secrecy in protecting product inventions, but less effective on process inventions.

2.4. The role of patent licensing

Inventors or the corporations for whom they work, and to whom they assign their patents, can use patents as a benefit appropriation mechanism either by commercializing the invention themselves, enjoying whatever degree of monopoly power patent protection provides, or by licensing their inventions to other firms and collecting an appropriate royalty. Licensing poses a variety of strategic problems. On one hand, when firms both exploit the invention themselves and license it to others, there is a danger that the licensee will be more skilled, or luckier, in marketing the resulting product or perfecting the invention's technical development than they were as original inventors. In this respect, licensing may confer upon rivals potential strategic advantages. On the other hand, the possibility that a licensee will make further improvements in the invention means that the licensor may be able to extend its own technology farther than it would if no licenses were conferred. Alternatively, patents may in any event provide only weak protection against parallel or duplicative inventions by rivals. In both of these cases, licensing may be seen as a desirable strategy because it allows the patent holder to extract a quid pro quo of access to other firms' technology as well as royalties for the use of its own technology. It may also create a basis (subject to antitrust law restrictions) for agreements to restrict competition among the firms, e.g., by setting common prices or dividing up the market. Given these conflicting possibilities, will patent holders license, or not?

A particularly comprehensive West German survey revealed that companies are reluctant to license their "core" technology, but they do readily license the technology on derivative products and on secondary product lines [60, pp. 52–54, 60–64, 141, and 149]. Another way of realizing the benefits of licensing while avoiding the risks is to extend limited licenses—e.g., confining licensees to non-competing products or geographic market areas. A special case of the non-competing market area strategy is to license only companies operating in the same product line overseas not those who compete domestically. Caves *et al.* [27] distinguished the licensing practices of "dominant product firms," that is, 60 percent of whose sales depended upon a single product, and those of "large diversified" companies, which were less dependent upon a single line. Among the dominant product firms in their sample, 85 percent of the patent licenses were concluded with foreign producers. For the more diversified companies, on the other hand, only 65 percent of licenses went to foreign companies.

When direct competitors are licensed, it is common that the parties obtain grant-back licenses, providing access to existing and follow-on inventions of the cross-licensing firms [27, p. 271]. Telesio [167, pp. 93–103] found that among multinational corporations, reciprocal licensing was associated with several characteristics. In particular, companies that did engage in reciprocal licensing tended to have higher R&D/sales ratios and higher levels of diversification than firms that did not. The multinational reciprocal licensors were also concentrated with special frequency in the pharmaceutical, other chemical, and electrical fields.

Licenses to like companies abroad may also be extended as a substitute for direct foreign investment. Because of relatively fixed information-gathering and startup costs in establishing an overseas operation, firms expecting to gain a large foreign market share face lower unit entry costs in making direct foreign investment than firms expecting relatively small shares. To the extent that these expectations are correlated with domestic market size, extending the geographic scope of one's patents through overseas licensing tends to be more attractive for small firms than for large companies. The licensing vs. direct foreign investment choice is also influenced by the costs of transferring technology between firms. Teece [166] found that technology transfer costs ranged from 2 to 59 percent of the total project costs falling on the foreign licensee, with an average value of 26 percent. When technology transfers at arms length are costly, firms are more apt to exploit their technology overseas through direct investment, all else equal.

Because competitors are often able to "invent around" one's patents, because litigation against a firm challenging the validity of patents is costly, and because cross-licensing and reciprocal transfer agreements bring non-monetary benefits, the royalties charged for patent use tend for the most part to be modest. See [27, 106, 164]. Royalty rates tend to lie in the range of 1 to 10 percent of sales, with an average of 3 to 4 percent. Typically, licensors tend to appropriate through royalties not more than a third to a half of the benefits realized by licensees from the use of patented inventions.

3. THE PURE THEORY OF PATENT PROTECTION

Over the years, the economic theory of how patent protection affects inventor behavior and how those responses in turn can affect the choices of patent policy-makers has seen rich theoretical development. We now explore the main contours of that literature. At first, the fact that patents and licenses vary in their effectiveness at preventing duplication and appropriating for the inventor the benefits from invention will be ignored. It will be assumed counter-factually that the patent is a highly effective, if not perfect, instrument of appropriation. Modifications more in line with the empirical evidence on patents and patent licensing will be introduced at a later stage in the argument.

3.1. The Nordhaus model

We begin with the pioneering model of optimal patent life introduced in 1967 by William Nordhaus [119, 120, pp. 70–90]. Nordhaus' fairly intricate mathematical presentation is followed only to the extent that clear exposition requires. Otherwise, we rely upon Scherer's geometric representation [144].

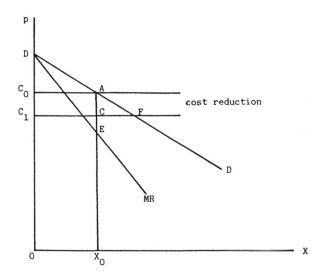

FIGURE 1   Determination of the optimal royalty (run-of-the-mill case).

Although the results can be extended to product inventions, Nordhaus focuses on cost-reducing production process inventions. He assumes a perfectly competitive industry that produces some product at constant units costs C_0 [Figure 1]. Price is OC_0 and output is OX_0. The inventor (or more realistically, inventing firm) devises a process that reduces costs from C_0 to C_1. If the inventor charges a price slightly lower than OC_0, it drives competitors out of the industry and becomes a monopolist. Its monopoly profits then are slightly smaller than the rectangle $C_0 C_1 CA$. Alternatively, the inventor can license the patented process to its existing competitors. Assuming that the would-be licensees have no alternative (i.e., circumventing) invention possibilities and assuming also zero transaction costs, the highest per-unit royalty that can be charged is the unit cost reduction $C_0 C_1$. The corresponding royalty rate as a percentage of product's price is $B = (C_0 - C_1)/C_0$. The inventor maximizes its profits from the invention by licensing it at the royalty rate B and receiving the full rectangle $C_0 C_1 CA$ in royalties. At this royalty rate, the post-invention price and output will remain unchanged relative to the pre-invention levels. For all cost reductions in the interval between A and E, the maximum royalty rate extractable is identical to the percentage rate of cost reduction. These cost-reducing inventions, for which the post-invention price–output combination remains unchanged from the pre-invention set, are called "non-drastic" or "run-of-the-mill" inventions. However, for inventions reducing costs below the level at which the market's marginal revenue function cuts a vertical at the pre-invention output, i.e., at point E, the profit-maximizing post-invention output will be larger, and the post-invention price lower, than in the pre-invention situation. This is so whether the inventor chooses to set that lower price and drive others out of the market, monopolizing the market itself, or license competitors at a royalty approximating the difference between the new profit-maximizing price and the new level of unit costs. Such output-expanding inventions, which occur when very large cost reductions are achieved and/or demand is especially elastic, are called "drastic" inventions by Nordhaus. We focus here mainly on the non-drastic or "run of the mill" invention case.

Non-drastic inventions yield royalty income per period of $v = X_0(C_0 - C_1)$. Normalizing the price P_0 to equal 1, the percentage royalty rate is $B = 1 - C_1$ and total royalties per period are $v = BX_0$. Assuming stationary demand over time and no appearance of competing inventions, royalties remain at the level v for the T periods (beginning at time 0) during which the patent is in force. With a discount rate of r per unit of time, the discounted present value of the royalty stream is:

$$V = \int_0^T BX_0 e^{-rt}\,dt = (BX_0/r)(1 - e^{-rt}). \tag{1}$$

Letting $\psi(t) = 1 - e^{-rt}$ and integrating, this simplifies to:

$$V = \psi BX_0/r. \tag{2}$$

Since X_0 is constant for non-drastic inventions, V is a linear function of B at any given patent life T. A parametric change in the patent life T rotates the V function from the origin 0 to the left or right. See Figure 2. If the discount rate r were 0, a doubling of the patent life would lead to a doubling of the present value V associated with any given cost reduction B. However, at positive discount rates, any given year's quasi-rents $v = BX_0$ are discounted more heavily, the

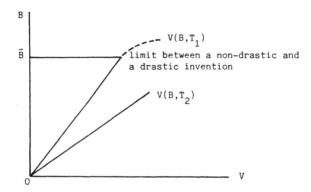

FIGURE 2 Present values of alternative cost reductions B at given patent lives $T_1 < T_2$.

more distant is their occurrence in the future. Thus, increases in the patent life lead to less than proportional rightward shifts in the discounted present value function V. For cost reduction values B sufficiently large to make the invention "drastic," the present value function V is nonlinear, bending to the right at values of B above those at which the transition from "run of the mill" to "drastic" status occurs.

To carry the analysis beyond a linking of discounted rewards to the extent of invention and the length of the patent's life, Nordhaus postulates the existence of an "invention possibility function" IPF, which relates the amount of cost reduction B achieved to the amount of money R spent on cost-reducing research and development. Thus, $B = \beta R^{\alpha}$, with $\beta > 0$ and $\alpha < 1$. The inventor's profits are therefore the surplus of the discounted present value of the quasi-rents from invention V minus R&D costs R:

$$\pi = V - R = \psi B X_0 / r - R. \qquad (3)$$

The first order condition for the inventor's profit maximum is:

$$\partial \pi / \partial R = \psi B' X_0 - 1 = 0, \qquad (4)$$

or rewritten,

$$\psi B' X_0 = r. \qquad (5)$$

This says that the inventor maximizes profits by extending its R&D efforts until the cost reduction benefit resulting from spending an

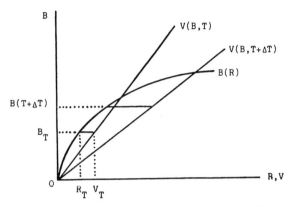

FIGURE 3   Impact of patent life extension on the profit-maximizing cost-reducing
invention.

additional dollar on R&D is equal to the interest carrying cost of
that dollar. Figure 3 brings the two sides of the inventor's problem
together. $V(B, T)$ is the present value function for a given patent
life T, while $B(R)$ is the invention possibility function. Profits are
maximized with a cost reduction of magnitude B_T, where the V and
B functions have equal slopes. The impact of an extension of the
patent life T by ΔT is now easily seen. The V function is shifted to
the right, inducing the inventor to exert more R&D effort,
achieving maximum profits with a cost reduction of magnitude
$B(T + \Delta T)$.

The patent life T is viewed as a parameter by the inventor.
However, for the government, it is a policy variable. Nordhaus'
wedge into the government's policy problem is the assumption that,
by letting prices remain above the levels consistent with post-
invention marginal production costs, a dead-weight welfare loss
(shown by triangle ACF in Figure 1) is incurred during the patent's
life. When the patent expires, prices fall (instantaneously) to the
level of post-invention costs C_1, the dead-weight welfare loss is
eliminated, and what had been producer's surplus (i.e., the
inventor's royalty) v is transformed into consumers' surplus.
(Redistributional effects associated with possibly differing marginal
utilities of income are ignored.)

In the simplest Nordhaus-type model, the patent policy-maker
seeks to set an optimal patent life T^* that maximizes the surplus of
the benefits to society, i.e., producers and consumers, from cost

reduction, minus the R&D costs necessary for cost reduction, all subject to the fact that the inventor responds to any given T in a profit-maximizing way. The benefits to society of a non-drastic invention are the cost saving C_0C_1CA (realized by the producer as profits from time 0 to time T, and by consumers as consumers' surplus from time T to infinity) plus the triangular area ACF realized as consumers' surplus from time T to infinity as competition drives prices to the new lower cost, and output expands. Call these two benefits W_1 and W_2 respectively. Nordhaus shows that:

$$W_1 + W_2 = \psi BX_0/r + B(X_1 - X_0)(1 - \psi)/2r. \tag{6}$$

To maximize welfare subject to the inventor's profit-maximizing behavior constraint (Eq. (5)), one forms the Lagrangian function:

$$U = W_1 + W_2 - R + \lambda(\psi B'X_0 - r). \tag{7}$$

This function is differentiated with respect to ψ and R. Assuming a specific form for the Invention Possibility Function $B = \beta R^\alpha$, and carrying out manipulations too complex to reproduce here, Nordhaus obtains the first order maximization conditions:

$$\psi = \frac{\eta B + 1}{\eta B(1 + \sigma/2) + 1}, \tag{8a}$$

$$T^* = -(1/r)\ln(1 - \psi), \tag{8b}$$

where η is the price elasticity of demand, and $\sigma = (1 - \alpha)/\alpha$ measures the Invention Possibility Function's curvature. Since α is the elasticity of output (i.e., cost reduction B) with respect to R&D input, high values of σ, that is, low values of α, imply an inelastic cost reduction response to incremental R&D changes. At the limit, $\sigma = \infty$ implies an L-shaped IPF, analogous to a Leontief production function isoquant. Although Eqs (8a) and (8b) are difficult to simplify further, it can be seen that the welfare-maximizing patent life T^* is shorter:

a) the larger is the price elasticity of demand η;

b) the greater is the equilibrium amount of cost reduction B (i.e., the "easier" invention is);

c) the larger the time discount rate r is; and

d) the smaller the elasticity of cost reduction α is with respect to R&D input, that is, the larger σ.

For the most part, these results have a clear intuitive rationale. What drives the Nordhaus model is an assumed tradeoff between more cost reduction from a longer patent life on the one hand and a longer-lasting deadweight loss burden (triangle ACF) on the other hand. Assuming linear demand, the formula for the deadweight loss triangle is $\eta B^2 S/2$, where S represents total sales of the industry's product. For given S, the deadweight loss triangle increases in magnitude linearly with increases in the price elasticity η and quadratically with increases in the equilibrium cost reduction B. This burden is borne only until the patent expires. Both before and after the patent expires, society benefits by the cost reduction rectangle $C_0 C_1 CA$. With the benefits from more cost reduction increasing linearly with B but the deadweight loss burden increasing quadratically with B, it makes sense to sacrifice some cost reduction at the margin to ensure that the deadweight loss is terminated early (i.e., with a lower value of T^*). Since the cost reduction rectangle is not affected by price elasticity η, at least for non-drastic inventions, but since the deadweight loss triangle increases linearly with η, an earlier termination of the deadweight loss burden is warranted, the larger that burden is owing to larger η. In the extreme case of zero demand elasticity, there is no deadweight loss and the optimal patent life is infinite.

Solving equations (8a) and (8b) assuming a discount rate r of 0.20 and (from empirical work by others, see [61, 99, and 110]) an elasticity of substitution σ of 0.10, Nordhaus finds that the optimal patent life in run-of-the-mill invention cases ranges from 15.8 years, for equilibrium cost reductions of 1 percent with a demand elasticity of unity, to 4.2 years for cost reductions of 10 percent and demand elasticity of 2.0, to 1.8 years for cost reductions of 50 percent and demand elasticity of 2.0.

The welfare-maximizing patent life increases with reductions in the time discount rate r because, at lower r, society discounts less, i.e., places more weight on, the increased benefits received after the patent expires and competition eliminates the deadweight loss triangle burden. This formulation assumes that inventor firms and the government (as patent policy-maker and overseer of general welfare) share the same discount rate. If private firms' discount rates exceed the socially optimal rate, e.g., because of risk aversion, tax wedges, and/or capital market imperfections, a given patent life will stimulate less cost reduction, all else equal, because the quasi-rents realized will be discounted more heavily. With lower resulting values of B, patent policy-makers will compensate by raising T^* at the margin.

A high elasticity of cost reduction α, that is, a low value of σ, implies that a given increment of R&D effort leads to relatively large incremental cost reductions, and therefore relatively long patent lives are warranted, all else equal. In the opposite case, where $\alpha \to 0$ and $\sigma \to \infty$, increases in R&D yield no incremental cost reduction, in which case, Nordhaus shows for invention possibility functions of the form $B = \beta R^\alpha$, the welfare-maximizing patent life will be zero. However, Scherer [114] points out that this is a special and perhaps improbable case. Suppose that IPF is L-shaped. For example, R&D expenditures up to $5 million are insufficient to complete any cost reduction project. Once the $5 million threshold has been achieved, a 10 percent cost reduction can be effected. But because of rigidities in the technological possibilities, expenditures above $5 million will not lead to further cost reductions. These assumptions imply a σ of ∞ where the IPF corners at R&D = $5 million. However, a zero patent life is not warranted, since with zero patent life, given the assumption of instantaneous post-patent imitation, the inventor will appropriate no rewards and hence will make no R&D investment. The optimal patent life in this case is one that shifts the benefits function $V(B, T)$ in Figure 3 enough to the right to permit the inventor to expect discounted quasi-rents just sufficient to cover its R&D costs. Thus, as Scherer urges, patent grants have two functions. One is to get the *marginal* conditions for welfare maximization (equations (8a) and (8b)) right, stimulating incremental R&D efforts whose costs at the margin equal marginal discounted social benefits. This is what the Nordhaus theory emphasizes. The second function is to assure inventors that at the optimum, the *total* conditions for profit maximization are satisfied, i.e., that the inventor's expected quasi-rents are greater than or (at worst) equal to expected R&D and other investment costs.

"Drastic" inventions are more complex mathematically. As Nordhaus [119] shows, the first-order conditions do not lend themselves to straightforward interpretation. Nordhaus' numerical evaluations reveal that, depending upon the specific parameter configurations, both very short and very long patent lives can be optimal. These difficulties may explain why he excluded analysis of the drastic case from the book version of his work [120].

The Nordhaus model assumes that, after achieving its patented cost reduction, the inventor charges either the single monopoly profit-maximizing price (in the drastic case) or keeps the end product price at the cost level associated with previous, now inferior, technologies. In other words, no price discrimination is practiced. Assume however that the patent-holder implements a royalty rate scheme permitting first-degree price discrimination with respect to consumers having reservation prices in the interval $C_0 > P > C_1$. Then what in the Nordhaus model is deadweight welfare loss until the patent expires becomes producer's surplus— perhaps shared by the patent-holder and its licensees. With no deadweight loss, and again assuming no distributive distinction between benefits to consumers and benefits captured by producers, the welfare-maximizing patent life becomes infinite. This is so because in the Nordhaus model, it is only to avoid the deadweight loss burden that patent lives are set to provide less than the maximum stimulus to cost reduction.

3.2. Optimal patents with compulsory licensing

We proceed now to relax some of the more restrictive assumptions in the Nordhaus model. One is the assumption that during the life of its patent, the inventor is sufficiently insulated from competition and transaction costs that it can license its invention at a royalty appropriating the full cost savings afforded by the new over the pre-invention technology. This might not be true if the patent-holder were compelled to license its technology to all seekers at a "reasonable" royalty, defined here, as in common practice, to be one lower than the full surplus-appropriating royalty. Many national patent statutes include provisions for compulsory licensing under certain (usually quite limited) circumstances, and, it will be recalled, the possibility of compulsory licensing was advanced during the 19th Century as a telling argument against the anti-patent movement.

Tandon [163] was the first to analyze formally the logic of compulsory licensing in a model that otherwise follows Nordhaus.

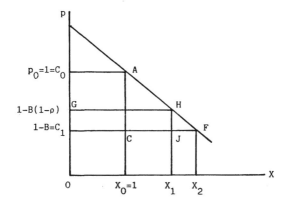

FIGURE 4   Royalty determination under compulsory licensing.

He posed the problem as one of making a two-dimensional policy choice: setting an optimal patent life, as in the Nordhaus model, but also setting an optimal royalty rate to be charged to otherwise unrestricted licensees. By setting the royalty rate below the rate the patent holder would charge if not so constrained, the policy-maker allows competition to drive the post-invention price below the pre-invention price and thereby lessens the deadweight loss sustained. This action reduces the inventor's quasi rents and hence its incentive to innovate, but by increasing the patent life, the policy-maker can compensate at least in part.

Figure 4 follows Figure 1, but adds the effects of compulsory licensing. To simplify the notation, pre-invention prices, unit costs, and output have all been normalized so that $C_0 = P_0 = 1$ and $X_0 = 1$. An invention reduces costs to C_1. But the inventor is not allowed to extract the whole percentage cost reduction B from its licensees. Rather, it may only charge a fraction $\rho < 1$ of the full cost reduction; i.e., the compulsory license royalty is set at ρB. Thus, immediately after the invention is put into practice, the end product price drops from OC_0 to OG, or normalized, to $1 - B(1 - \rho)$, covering licensees' unit costs $1 - B$ plus the license royalty ρB. Output expands to X_1. Relative to the pre-invention situation, social benefits, i.e., the sum of inventor's and consumers' surplus, are increased immediately by $A_1 = C_0AHJC_1$. The present value of this increment is A_1/r. Adapting equation (3) to these new conditions, the inventor's profit equation is:

$$\pi = V - R = (\psi \rho B X_1 / r) - R. \tag{9}$$

Since the new output level X_1 can be shown, given the normalizations adopted earlier, to be $1 + \rho B(1 - \rho)$, this can be rewritten:

$$\pi = (\psi/r)\rho B(1 + \eta B(1 - \rho)) - R. \tag{10}$$

The first order condition for profit maximization becomes:

$$\partial \pi / \partial R = \psi \rho B'(1 + 2\eta B(1 - \rho)) = r. \tag{11}$$

The expression $\rho(1 + 2\eta B(1 - \rho))$ is the marginal revenue product of an additional dollar spent on cost reduction. Let it be denoted as M. Then the inventor's equilibrium condition simplifies to:

$$\psi B' M = r, \tag{12}$$

which differs from equation (5) earlier in the substitution of marginal revenue product for the fully appropriate royalty.

After the patent expires in T years, the end product's price falls all the way to the level of cost $1 - B$; rectangle GC_1JH is transformed from inventor's to consumers' surplus; and additional consumers' surplus measured by deadweight loss triangle HJF, denoted by A_2, is realized. The policy maker maximizes the Lagrangian function:

$$Z = A_1/r + A_2(1 - \psi)/r - R + \lambda((\psi/r)B'M - 1) \tag{13}$$

with respect to ψ, ρ, and λ. The derivations are complex and will be omitted. Tandon shows that if, at the optimal compulsory royalty rate ρ^*, the derivative $\partial Z/\partial \psi > 0$, then ψ must be raised to its maximum value of 1, which occurs only with an infinite patent life. Thus, with optimal compulsory licensing, the reduction in incentive is compensated by extending the optimal patent life to perpetuity! If for some reason the patent's life is set at a lower (finite) value, the royalty rate must be adjusted upward to compensate. Given an infinite patent life, the optimal royalty rate is lower:

a) the larger the price elasticity η is;

b) the larger the equilibrium amount of cost reduction B, which in turn implies greater ease of invention; and

c) the smaller the cost reduction elasticity α is with respect to R&D inputs, that is, the larger σ.

The intutition underlying these results is the same as for the Nordhaus model discussed previously.

3.3. Competition, imperfect patents, and rent seeking

The Nordhaus-Tandon models imply a peculiarly secure inventing firm. At the time it makes its invention, it is the only firm exploiting a given Invention Possibility Function. After invention but during the patent's life, it in effect "owns" the relevant technology and can appropriate royalties, full or whittled down by "reasonable" compulsory licensing, from all users. Only after the patent expires does the inventing firm experience direct competition.

A modification of these restrictive assumptions requires recognition that competition can occur at any or all of three stages: before the invention is made and/or patented, after invention but before the patent expires, and after the patent expires. These might be called Stage I, Stage II, and Stage III competition respectively. Again, in the Nordhaus model, competition occurs only during Stage III. Not surprisingly, introducing competition into Stages I and II changes the derived implications, in some instances radically.

Competition in Stage II is in some respects analogous to the compulsory licensing case analyzed previously. If several patented processes exist, each patented by a separate firm, competition among the patent owners is likely to reduce the royalty rate any given patent holder can charge below the rate that fully appropriates the cost savings attainable relative to pre-invention technologies. See [16 and 106]. Competitors' challenges to the legal validity of a firm's patent can have the same effect; given the costs and risks of litigation, the patent holder may be better off settling out-of-court for a less-than-maximum royalty rate. In either case, ignoring for the moment the costs that may have been incurred to create Stage II competition, welfare-maximizing patent lives may have to be increased to compensate for the reduction in inventors' royalty income and hence the weakening of incentives to invent.

Competition during pre-patent Stage I poses more difficult analytic problems. Under the Nordhaus model assumptions, a single firm in effect has a monopoly at this stage. The polar alternative, attributable originally to Barzel [11], is to assume that pure competition prevails, so that a host of firms compete for the legal right to obtain *the* patent and hence to monopolize Stage II. Under pure competition, "rent-seeking" firms [4, 14, 79, 128] will compete so vigorously for that right that the expected profits from invention will be driven to zero. This can occur in three main ways. First, as Barzel argued [11], the costs of invention fall over time as scientific knowledge and/or technology advance exogenously, or the prospective benefits from invention may rise over time as demand grows. The earlier investment is made in a specific inventive possibility, the higher will be the cost, or the lower will be the immediately appropriable quasi-rents, leading in either case to falling profitability with earlier invention. Under pure competition, the winner of an ongoing auction to be the first and hence winning inventor will undertake its inventive effort so early that, because of high R&D costs or low expected quasi-rents or both, it will just break even. Second, and contrary to the assumptions of both the Nordhaus and Barzel models, inventions can seldom be made and developed instantaneously. It takes time to carry out the necessary R&D. And as Scherer showed [141, 142], for a given starting point in time, the more rapidly the R&D effort proceeds, the higher will be the total costs of carrying out the R&D project. Thus, competitive acceleration of R&D schedules as well as competitive acceleration of the date at which R&D commences will raise costs, squeezing competitive inventors' expected profits to zero under pure competition. Third, it may happen that the winner of an R&D—patenting race realizes positive profits, but firms losing the race incur losses, so on average, before the winner is determined, the expected value of profits for the collection of all firms competing in Stage I is zero. Indeed, if the competitors are homogeneous, so that none has an advantage in inventing over the others, and if the competitors correctly calculate the probabilities, pure competition will force them to accelerate their inventive efforts and carry the amount of cost reduction they seek to achieve so far that the expected value of profits for any given competitor is zero.[8]

From the standpoint of a patent policy-maker striving to maximize social welfare, it matters little which, or what combination, of

---

[8] This assumes that firms maximize the expected value of their profits. If they are risk averse, the acceleration will not be carried as far, and positive profits may remain for the group. Individual firms may also view their rivalry as subject to a "winner's curse," in which case, under certain models, an intensification of competition will lead to lower spending on R&D.

these scenarios holds. Pure competition among rent-seeking firms at the pre-patent stage drives costs up until their total amount is equivalent to V of equation (2), that is, to the discounted present value of the recurring rectangles $C_0 C_1 CA$ in Figure 1, assuming complete monopoly for the winner during Stage II. In the Nordhaus model, those rectangles were producer's surplus and hence a social gain during Stage II. In the limiting purely competitive case, the surplus is more or less exactly offset by rent-seeking costs. Consequently, what was in the Nordhaus model a benefit to society, whose realization was worth suffering dead-weight losses over an extended patent life, is obliterated by costs incurred to win the prize. In the limiting case, the only benefit remaining for society is the gain in consumers' surplus measured by trapezoid $C_0 C_1 FA$ in Figure 1, whose realization begins only when the patent expires and continues (by assumption) in perpetuity. Shorter patent lives permit that gain to be realized earlier, but shorter patent lives also reduce the cost reduction stimulus to rent-seeking competitors, and thus they reduce the size of the trapezoid once it is finally realized. With early rectangular gain $C_0 C_1 CA$ offset fully by R&D costs, the nature of this tradeoff changes dramatically. Since the only benefits to society come after the patent's life has ended, short patent lives will prove optimal. As McFetridge and Rafiquzzaman [106] have demonstrated, optimal patent lives are both quite short and insensitive to parameter changes. For a discount rate of ten percent and an elasticity of the IPF of 0.10, Nordhaus found the optimal patent life with his run-of-the-mill model to be 31.6 years for a cost reduction of 10 percent and a demand elasticity of unity, or 8.5 years with the same cost reduction and a demand elasticity of 2.0. But in the pure rent-seeking case analyzed by McFetridge and Rafiquzaman, the optimal patent life remains unchanged at 1.1 years!

One way to deal with the rent-seeking problem is to accept it and adjust "optimal" (now, actually third-best) patent lives accordingly. Another way is to attempt to prevent it from happening.

In an influential paper, Kitch [75, 76] has argued that patent grants are exclusive rights to "prospect" in a field of technology, and hence to keep others out of the area. Firms are assumed to obtain basic patents staking out the field, and once that position is achieved, the patent right is used to prevent other firms from performing rent-seeking research and development that would otherwise dissipate the surpluses associated with achievable inventions.

The Kitch view suffers from two major debilities, one theoretical and one empirical. See [14, 15, 105, and 147, p. 451]. For one, granting patents as exclusive rights to prospect in a field of technology merely pushes rent-seeking competition to an earlier stage. Under such a system, firms will incur expenditures to win the original prospect-defining patent, and if their foresight is good and their competition strong, these expenditures will rise to dissipate most or all of the rents from post-prospect inventions. Also, the evidence available suggests that few if any actual patents are sufficiently basic, and confer sufficiently strong exclusionary rights, to give their holder an unchallenged position in developing a field of technology. In this respect, Kitch's terminology, chosen by analogy from the field of mineral property rights, was perhaps better-justified than intended, for studies of the Western United States mining rights reveal that "claims" staked out under the prospector's rights system often overlap in complex and multiple ways, leading to extensive litigation when firms actually undertake to develop the properties. See [44, pp. 657–674]. It is true that some firms have enjoyed patent positions sufficiently strong to discourage entry into a technological field. See e.g. [19] on the case of xerography. But most commonly, those positions are defended by patent portfolios containing dozens or even hundreds of patents, not one, and the field-defining patents were accumulated over many years of development work, not from a single initial prospect patent.

The pure Stage I rent-seeking case is the sort of extreme upon which precise theorizing can be done. It is sometimes approximated crudely in the real world, but it is absent with at least equal frequency. Indeed, in many cases, rather than being a race to the patent office, invention consists of a lonely struggle to perfect an invention and have its merits recognized both by the patent office and the market.

Assuming pure Nordhausian monopoly in post-invention Stage II also misrepresents what is in reality a complex mixture of monopoly, competition, and in-between variants. As noted earlier, patents seldom confer iron-clad exclusionary rights. This is shown inter alia by the evidence that royalties seldom appropriate the full

benefit provided by an invention. More commonly, the appropriation fraction is in the range of 20 to 50 percent. See [106, pp.
105–108]. This reduces the incentive of individual inventors, nudg-
ing optimal patent lives upward if the result of weaker incentives is
less cost reduction and also lengthening optimal patent lives if the
consequence is less wastefully duplicative rent-seeking.[9]

The real world is some unknown blend of these tendencies, which
without further information suggests that optimal patent lives ought
to lie somewhere between the extremes indicated by the Nordhaus
and Tandon models on one hand and the pure rent-seeking theories
on the other. Applying empirically plausible demand elasticities,
Invention Possibility Function parameters, degrees of rent seeking,
and appropriable cost reduction benefit fractions to a composite
model, McFetridge and Rafiquzzaman [106] derive optimal patent
lives roughly five times longer than those found for the pure
rent-seeking case. Arguing that McFetridge and Rafiquzzaman
overestimate the amount of rent seeking, e.g., by not taking into
account the impact of uncertainty and future technological change,
Beck [16] finds it reasonable to extend patent lives even further.

Even with this narrowing of the debate, the progress that has
been made thus far is incomplete. Three loose ends remain.

For one, duplication of inventive activities by rent-seeking firms is
not necessarily bad. When the probability that any single approach
will lead to success is low, duplication permits a desirable acceleration of technological progress, or the achievement of higher-quality
inventions than what would otherwise emerge. See e.g. [7, 37, 69,
70, 78, 89, 124, 131, and 141]. Duplication also helps ensure that
important technological approaches are not overlooked. For instance, Burton, the inventor of the batch process of petroleum

---

[9] The patent system may generate simultaneous competition in Stages I and II
when firms are induced to "invent around" any given firm's patent, e.g., because
excessive royalty payments are demanded or firms have a "not invented here" bias
against rival inventions. This can lead both to socially wasteful duplication and the
introduction of inferior technologies. For example, when the generally available
technology involves production costs of $10 per unit, Firm A may invent a process
that reduces costs to $7 per unit. Suppose Firm B can invent an inferior substitute
process with unit costs of $8.50. If Firm A attempts to charge the $3.00 royalty
consistent with the generally available technology, or indeed any royalty exceeding
$1.50, Firm B will develop and use its process, even though from a broader
viewpoint, economic efficiency suffers.

"cracking," resisted the idea of continuous cracking, but work by other inventors showed that the continuous approach was superior. [41, pp. 52–53] The difficult part comes in determining how much duplication is socially optimal.

Second, conducting multiple R&D projects in a given field of technology not only accelerates progress, but leads to a diversity of inventions and technological solutions, each of which, especially in the case of product inventions, has advantages in satisfying the diverse tastes of different consumers. Models examining the question of optimal product variety show that it is possible under plausible conditions for there to be too few competitive approaches, too many, or just the right amount, with no guarantee that the third result will dominate. See [146, 157]. That the results of these relatively narrowly-focused analyses can be so ambiguous is in itself disconcerting. In addition, little progress has been made to date in integrating the work on optimal product variety with the theories of optimal patent life and strength. Thus, much remains to be learned.

Finally, all of the extant formal theories assume that patent protection is the only means by which imitators are prevented from competing away the inventor's appropriated benefits. In truth, as [86], [145], and [164] show, there are other barriers to competitive imitation, and much R&D would occur even if no patent system existed. In simple form, the assumption that patents are the only barrier to imitation can be relaxed by assuming that after the patent expires, prices do not fall instantaneously to the competitive level. Both the increased incentive to inventors and the delayed realization of the full consumers' surplus benefits from invention under these revised assumptions imply a movement in the direction of shorter lives. Since non-patent barriers to entry may also help sustain profit levels that in themselves induce additional rent-seeking, patent lives again may have to be reduced to compensate. However, more complicated scenarios have not been studied, nor have models been developed to examine interactions between patent and non-patent barriers to imitation. Again, much work remains to be done.

Models of firm behavior under the patent system have also been extended to cover the case in which incumbent, dominant firms perpetuate their positions of dominance by preemptive patenting. See [25, 49, 50, 51, 71, 131, and 132]. The preemption theories' realism is open to question. If non-patent barriers to entry are important, the threats of outside inventors will be less credible, and so efforts to preempt them will be less likely. Also, the persistence of patent-based monopoly positions may be explained as much by what Kahn calls "patent diplomacy" as by aggressive preemptive patenting [68, p. 328]. That is, incumbent firms bolster their positions behind a formidable portfolio of patents by acquiring the patents, or all the assets, of new firms who have made, or appear about to make, relevant inventions. Preemption may also fail because the incumbent firm is lulled by its superiority into thinking that significant challenges will not succeed, only to be taken by surprise by some outsider unwilling, after a foothold has been secured, to surrender its independence through merger. That such failures occur is demonstrated by the high share of radically new products and processes contributed by new entrant firms. See [1; 47; 66; 147, p. 438; and 159].

4. THE PRO AND CONTRA OF PATENT PROTECTION

The basic idea behind the patent grant is to combat what would otherwise be a tendency toward under-investment in research, development, and related activities. Under-investment can occur because inventions are in important respects like public goods, making it difficult for the inventor to appropriate their benefits, and because of the uncertainties pervading inventive activity [5, 6]. But even if patent protection proves to be highly effective in appropriating social benefits, it is a second-best solution, leaving prices in excess of costs during the patent's life and hence causing a misallocation of resources relative to the "first best" of inventions financed by minimally distorting taxes. When patents provide particularly strong protection in the post-invention period, they may also stimulate overinvestment in R&D as firms duplicate each others' inventive programs and accelerate them until inventions occur prematurely. Actual patents seldom qualify as "prospects" in the strongly preclusive sense, and when they are circumvented easily, over-investment may take the form of extensive "inventing around" existing patents. Thus, imperfections in the patent system lead to both under-investment and over-investment in R&D.

occurring simultaneously and not necessarily in a mutually-canceling manner.

For activities as complex and uncertain as research, invention, and development, first-best solutions are utopian. A patent system may still be the best practical alternative. But what kind of patent system serves best? Ideally, each patent would be tailored to the supply and demand specifics of its underlying invention, so that just the right incentive is provided to stimulate the optimal amount of inventive effort. However, a patent system that attempts to treat each case individually is infeasible, among other things because no public authority could acquire the necessary information. Rather, decisions on the length and strength of patents must as a first approximation be made generally, not case-by-case.

At what parameter values that decision occurs depends upon how much invention will be lost if patent rights are weakened and how much inefficient rent-seeking behavior occurs under diverse circumstances. Here the Nordhaus model and its variants at least provide useful perspective. A uniform reduction of patent lives tends mainly to weed out inventions with low benefit potential (B in the Nordhaus model). Here too, however, the model may over-simplify. Especially in industries with rapid technological change, inventions tend to be cumulative, with each step in the inventive chain facilitating and setting the stage for inventions to follow. Each such invention then has a direct benefit associated with its immediate cost reduction (or product improvement) effect and in addition an indirect benefit associated with the follow-on inventions it makes possible. A general reduction in patent lives might therefore cause the loss not only of inventions with low direct benefit potential, but also the retardation of a whole sequence of inventions [177].

4.1. The social costs and benefits of the patent system

Despite these caveats, it is conceivable that the best general solution among imperfect alternatives would be patents with zero lives, i.e., no patent system at all. To see whether this might be true, we must consider in a more global way the costs and benefits of the system as it presently exists.

The social costs of the patent system are of two main kinds. There are administrative costs incurred by the government and patent recipients, and there are allocative costs in the form of static and dynamic inefficiencies caused by patents on inventions that would have been made without patent protection, or with less patent protection.

In 1981, the U.S. and West German Patent Offices had operating budgets of some $110 million and DM 200 million respectively. To these must be added the less easily ascertained expenditures for adjudication of patent disputes, company patent departments and the cost of independent patent counsel, and lobbying activities directed toward influencing patent policy. In a large industrialized nation, these costs may well add up to a billion dollars or more per year.

If a patent provides more protection than is necessary to induce the desired invention or innovation, the patentee can extract larger price-cost margins, imposing dead-weight losses, and those may persist for too long a period. Perhaps even more important than these first-order costs [68] are the second- and third-order costs arising when the patent induces inefficient rent-seeking, restrains the innovative efforts of others, and/or interacts with other entry barriers to cement monopolistic market positions. Normally, situations in which one firm's patents block another firm from innovating should be resolved by having each party cross-license rights to the other's patents. But cross licenses can also be used to fix prices and cartelize an industry, with quota assignments and entry restrictions that reduce efficiency, rather than improving it.[10] See also [22, 116, 117, 118, 169, and 174].

Although it is often easy to invent around one patent or a few, circumvention can become quite difficult if a technological field is blanketed by a whole patent portfolio held by a single firm or closely-coordinated cartel. The portfolio owner enjoys a monopsonistic demand position vis à vis outside inventors. As the most favored purchaser or licensor, it can offer less for their patents than they would be worth in a competitive market, and a result the outsiders' incentive to invent is reduced, which in turn allows the

---

[10] A leading U.S. antitrust case was *U. S. v. Line Material Co.,* 333 U.S. 287 (1948). Cross-licensing cases with price-fixing schemes in the United States included glass bottles, parking meters, eyeglasses, gypsum board, machine tools, magnesium, radio broadcasting equipment, and synthetic rubber, to name only a few. For further cases, see Vaughan [174, 105–167].

incumbent to slow down its own inventive effort or delay the introduction of existing inventions.[11] An example is found in the history of fluorescent lamps [23]. Although cases of outright suppression are rare, patents have been used more often to retard the exploitation of competing inventions. A financially strong patentee may also use its patents to threaten financially weaker inventors with infringement suits. Carboloy, a subsidiary of General Electric, brought numerous infringement suits against tungsten carbide rivals from 1930–40, intimidating them and imposing them pricing restraints. Carboloy was also able to avert or delay suits challenging the validity of its patents until 1940, when a court decision found them to be invalid.[12]

These abuses and their accompanying high social costs occur in conjunction with only a small minority of all patents. Most patents, it is clear inter alia from patentees' failure to pay renewal fees, have little value, either directly or in their contribution to portfolio effects. Using renewal data, Pakes and Schankerman [123] found that the average patent has an economic life of 4 years, with a confidence interval in the range of from 2.8 to 5.6 years. However, the distribution of patent values is highly skewed. The patent distribution has a long, thin tail made up of the relatively few patents of very high value. The distribution may in fact be so skewed that it is Paretian, with neither finite mean nor variance asymptotically [140, pp. 1097–1098]. Thus, to the extent that abuses exist (and probably only a small fraction of the high-valued patents are used in ways that might reasonably be called abusive), those exceptional cases might be dealt with specially-designed measures.

The costs associated with abuse and patent protection in excess of what is needed to call forth an efficient supply of inventions would be avoided if there were no patent system. But benefits would also be lost. How large might they be? The question is necessarily speculative. There are case studies identifying specific important inventions whose availability would probably have been delayed absent patent protection—e.g., Watt and his steam engine improvements, Farnsworth on television, and Carlson—Haloid on xero-

---

[11] See *Hartford-Empire Co. v. U. S.*, 323 U.S. 386 (1945); and *U. S. v. United Shoe Machinery Corp.*, 110 F. Supp. 295 (1953).

[12] *U. S. v. General Electric Co.*, 80 F. Supp. 989 (1948).

graphy. Although one must be wary of self-aggrandizing answers, questionnaire studies have provided convincing evidence that patents are important to research, development, and testing investments in certain broad fields such as pharmaceuticals. And they may provide valuable protection to smaller firms attempting to break down established positions with radically new concepts.

On a broader plane, Germany, Holland, and Switzerland provide examples in which industrialization occurred without national patent systems. In a case study of the Dutch and Swiss experience, Schiff [150] found no evidence that industrialization was hampered by the absence of patent protection. Yet this does not prove that patents are unimportant. It only shows that it may be advantageous for a less-developed nation to use inventions, stimulated perhaps by a patent system, from other nations. The French, British, and (later) German patent systems may have supplied important external benefits to neighbors without patent laws. In this respect, it is worth recalling that Switzerland introduced mechanical invention patents to protect its watch industry, but initially withheld patent protection on chemical substances and processes because its infant chemical industry relied upon imitating others' technology.

4.2. Alternatives to the patent system

If one were inclined toward eliminating the patent system but were unwilling to give up the inventions the system clearly stimulates, one must ask what alternative incentive mechanisms might be substituted. All industrialized nations have deployed a more or less broad array of non-patent measures to encourage, e.g., the development of weapons and space systems, specific civilian projects such as high-speed trains using the principle of supermagnetism, and agricultural research and development. The reasons for these auxiliary approaches vary. In some cases, the projects are thought to be so expensive and risky that they could not be drawn out, even with strong patent protection. Agricultural research and development is carried out by government laboratories and in government-subsidized university units because the atomistic structure of agriculture does not support R&D performed by farmers. (However, some agricultural R&D does thrive in industries supplying the farmers, such as in farm machinery, fertilizers, and foodstuffs.) Military hardware is procured through government-financed programs because the government must play an active role in defining its needs and because of the high costs and risks involved in pushing technological frontiers outward at the pace demanded by military buyers, who see themselves locked into a high-stakes arms race.

In cases like these, where the patent system fails, or is insufficient, the R&D resource allocation decision is centralized in government bureaucracies. But if this approach is substituted for patents generally, a critically important advantage is lost. Patents are especially useful in assisting those who pursue deviant ideas. When there is little disagreement concerning technical feasibility contract research may get the needed job done. But such research suffers from numerous principal—agent problems whose evaluation is beyond the scope of this paper. When special weight is placed on encouraging variety, the pursuit of novel and difficult-to-anticipate ideas, and a multiplicity of approaches, the patent system is almost surely superior to a centralized government contract solution. To be sure, substitutive inventive activity can be wasteful. But to determine ex ante the borderline between what is, and what is not, wasteful under conditions of substantial technical uncertainty is a task fraught with error. Patent stimuli do the job automatically, without resort to the fumbling bureaucratic hand.

Promising a prize for the delivery of a specific invention is an approach as ancient as the patent system.[13] See Wright [182]. Compared to contract research, the prize approach permits a greater variety of approaches and solutions. Prizes share this characteristic with patents. Even greater variety may be stimulated, since offering a prize publicizes the existence of an invention possibility to many potential inventors, whereas a patentable invention possibility may be overlooked by most. However, prizes

---

[13] A good example of a technological problem whose solution was encouraged through the offering of a prize was the measurement of longitude. The problem haunted ship navigators for centuries. In 1598, Philip III of Spain offered a cash prize of a thousand ducats plus a life annuity of two thousand ducats for a longitude-measuring invention. In 1713, the British Parliament passed an act offering a prize of 20,000 Pounds Sterling to the person who found a method of measuring longitude to an accuracy of one degree. The prize attracted the efforts of the greatest mathematicians, physicists, and instrument-makers (i.e., clock-makers) of their time. See [81, pp. 112, 145–147, 161–170].

focus attention upon the *invention* stage in the sequence from invention to commercialization, possibly leaving insufficient incentive for the subsequent investments needed to reduce inventions to practice. Patents are superior in this respect. Also, with both prizes and contract research, the precipitating bureaucracies are unlikely to command all the information needed consistently to recognize the convergence of technical opportunities on the supply side with unfilled demands, especially in undeveloped technical fields. In its speed at recognizing new possibilities and its hospitality to non-conformist ideas, the patent system copes more effectively with high levels of demand and supply uncertainty.

Instead of announcing a prize in advance for successfully mastering some well-specified invention possibility, government might grant awards after-the-fact, once inventions have been made in response to the inventor's own need perceptions. Inventors' certificates in the Soviet Union represent such an award system. The person who invents a cost reduction is entitled to a two percent share of the cost savings during the first five years of use, up to 20,000 rubles as a maximum. See [8, pp. 192–194; and 147, p. 458]. A common complaint, however, is that Soviet managers have a low propensity to introduce the inventions, even when they are available for the taking. Furthermore, such awards tend to have a narrow conception of inventive activity. Like the reward of employee inventions under Western law, inventors' certificates stress new ideas for improving production methods, but do not encourage the costly development and perfection of such ideas. Finally, there are complaints that cost savings estimates by official bodies are often faulty, and that awards tend to be modest, even in cases of exceptional creativity and ingenuity. Thus, awards, prizes, and contract research fail precisely where the patent system's comparative advantage lies—in stimulating the search for, and perfection of, radically new solutions.

4.3. The special problems of less-developed countries

Special problems concerning the patent system and its alternatives apply for less-developed countries. See [18, 28, 55, 58, 63, 65, 90, 125, 126, and 171]. Such nations tend to have relatively little domestic inventive activity, at least, judged at the levels required to satisfy international patentability standards. Most patents come from nations enjoying higher levels of economic development. The grant of patents to such outsiders by an LDC may help attract transfers of technology, augmented perhaps by direct investment in resident subsidiaries by multinational enterprises. To achieve such technology transfers, patents and patent licenses alone are almost surely insufficient. In addition, training and know-how transfers must occur. It is often asked why such transfers require the LDC to have its own patent law. Mightn't alternative contractual arrangements suffice? The answer, to the extent that a clear answer exists, may be that the presence of a domestic patent law is one of the several institutional elements required to create a climate of confidence sufficient to induce foreign corporation investment in technology transfer and on-site production.

The historical experience with industrialization in Holland, Germany, and Switzerland shows that it may initially be advantageous not to have a patent law, assuming that domestic inventive capabilities are sufficient to "free-ride" by imitating the technologies already developed by foreign enterprises. Only after industrialization has progressed further and technical skills have developed to a higher level does the nation introduce a national patent system to guide its domestic inventive activity away from imitation and toward more original work. China provides an example [90]. The patent law in force since April 1985 denies patentabilty for chemical substances and processes, but the Chinese government announced that once it has established viable chemical and pharmaceutical industries, it is willing to make the excluded inventions patentable. In this respect, China's policy closely replicates Switzerland's policy near the turn of the century. Both nations began by allowing patents in areas where they had an established industrial base, but Switzerland, like China, excluded chemical and pharmaceutical fields, where they were attempting to lay the basis for industrial development.

4.4. Approaches to reforming the patent system

If, as the weight of evidence seems to support, there is substantial merit in preserving a patent system for its value in inducing certain kinds of inventions, the question remains, might its working not be improved by introducing various reforms?

To discourage undesirable rent-seeking behavior, Beck [14, 15] proposes to augment the existing patent system by introducing a true prospect right, which would be auctioned off, the winner receiving exclusive rights to invent in a specified field to technology. In detail, his plan provides [15, p. 23]:

> Competitors must bid for a patent monopoly on the *anticipated* results of *future* research in order to eliminate incentives to compete unproductively. Before beginning research, any firm or individual could submit research objectives to the Patent Office as a definition of the patent to be awarded on payment of the highest bid. The maximum possible bid from each potential inventor would be that bidder's estimate of potential patent rent—the difference between expected royalty revenues and expected costs of invention. [emphasis in the original]

Presently, R&D results are patentable only if they have been proved experimentally. Beck would push patentability forward in time. Given the specification of not-yet-invented results, the inventor who knows the least-cost research method can submit the highest bid and will receive the patent. Unlike prospect systems under which inventors compete on the basis of actually achieved results, the bids are mere rent transfer payments from the winning inventor to the government, and hence should not distort resource allocation.

Nevertheless, several problems in such a system must be recognized. For one, bidding contests would not be feasible in areas of high technological uncertainty, where R&D results cannot be staked out in advance of actual work. Even if such claim staking were feasible, a research method that appears to be superior at the bidding stage might turn out to be inferior or even fruitless, so that the winner is not in fact the least-cost researcher. This problem might be remedied if the winner could license know-how from, or sell development rights to, other firms that, after the fact, turned out to possess superior inventive capabilities. But asymmetries in knowledge and bargaining power make such solutions difficult to achieve. Another disadvantage of prospect bidding might be a tendency to entrench the position of dominant firms. Under the present system, such firms can be taken by surprise if they rest on their technological oars, but under a prospect system, they would be able to scan all prospect proposals systematically and enter strong bids to preempt those that are strategically important.

Finally, invention and the innovative activities that follow it are processes in which learning plays a key role. "Duplicative" inven-

tive activity may be worthwhile not only because it lets a hundred
flowers bloom, but also because it keeps inventors experienced in
their trade and maintains their skills for making further technical
contributions in the future. In contrast, when a firm has won a
prospect patent, it alone accumulates technical experience in the
protected field, building a position in which it is also the most likely
winner of the next bidding round. Sooner or later, this concentra-
tion of technical skills may retard long-run competitiveness and
progress.

Another improvement suggested by many constructive critics is to
raise standards of patentability, screening out applications of
marginal inventiveness and/or economic value. One way to do so,
although not without substantial cost, is to increase the qualifica-
tions and number of patent examiners, so the tradeoff among speed
of decision, quality of decision, and fairness to applicants is slanted
more toward decision quality. An increase in patentability standards
might simultaneously be accompanied, as in Germany and other
nations, by the introduction of petty patents of narrower scope and
with shorter lives. A third way would be to introduce, or increase
the progressiveness over time of, patent maintenance fees, thereby
creating incentives to perform the weeding-out process themselves.
All such proposals would clear out the underbrush that impedes
passage through patent thickets. Yet none is likely to eliminate the
really important patents that define powerful market positions. And
steeply progressive maintenance fees might force financially weak
inventors to abandon patents before the underlying inventions were
developed sufficiently to establish their true value.

Because patents play a decisive incentive role in only a few
technological fields or niches, patentability might be restricted to
inventions in those areas. There are precedents for such discrimination. European patent law explicitly precludes patentability for
computer programs, and many nations exclude pharmaceutical or
foodstuff inventions from patentability. Yet such exclusions are
most often based upon legal syllogisms (i.e., the perceived
difference between computer software "inventions" and other
patentable matter) or upon the logic of free riding on other nations'
technological contributions. Attempting to limit patentability to
classes of inventions where the response of inventive effort to patent
protection is particularly elastic would break new ground. In

less-developed nations, for example, patents might be granted only on improved labor-intensive production methods, specially-adapted pesticides, and cures for tropical diseases.

Another way of channeling strong patent protection toward cases in which overall economic benefit is greatest would be to pursue selective compulsory licensing. The prospect of compulsory licensing, we recall, was influential in overcoming resistance from the anti-patent movement in the 19th Century. The first patent cooperation agreement of 1883 even provided that patents would lapse if they were not worked in the issuing nation. But in subsequent decades, that provision was gradually weakened and finally replaced by formulations under which governments could issue compulsory licenses if non-use of a patent injured the "public interest." More recently, the debate has shifted to less-developed countries.[14] At the 1981 Nairobi conference, a compromise was reached between industrialized and less-developed nations permitting LDCs to grant *exclusive* compulsory licenses if patent holders failed to utilize their inventions locally. Also, if non-use continued for five years, a patent might be revoked altogether. At later meetings, this compromise was rejected by the industrialized nations, with the United States taking the leading opposing position. As of 1987, all efforts to reach a new compromise had been unsuccessful.

The formal use of compulsory licensing is in practice fairly rare, both in less-developed nations and (with a few notable exceptions) in the industrialized lands. Statistics on the incidence of compulsory licensing under statutory mandates in a diversity of nations are assembled in Table II. Canada and Great Britain stand out as exceptions, mainly because they pursued active policies of enforcing compulsory licensing on patented pharmaceutical products, most of which (especially for Canada) were invented by foreign multinationals [54]. One reason for the characteristic paucity of compulsory licensing actions may be strict interpretation of the requirement that failure to work inventions domestically injure the public interest before a license can be granted. Another possible

---

[14] Actually, the LDCs' position has precedent in Venetian practice of the 15th century. In response to complaints by would-be users, patents not worked by their holders could be cancelled because "it is not suitable that the patent holder obstructs the work of others by not using his patents" ("non é conveniente cher per non operar loro (quei titolari), possino impedir l'opere d'altri." Cited in [97, p. 528].

ERICH KAUFER

TABLE II
Cases of compulsory licensing in diverse nations.

		Total Compulsory Licenses	
	Period covered	Requested	Granted
Industrialized nations			
Australia	1958–74	0	0
Denmark	1958–63	7	3
Canada	1935–59	45	9
	1960–74	183	117
France	1953–74	n.a.	3
Germany	1923–43	295	23
(West)	1950–79	37	0
United Kingdom	1950–72	121	31
Holland	1958–63	0	0
Ireland	1958–63	1	0
Japan	1960–74	12	0
Norway	1910–63	27	11
Switzerland	1952–63	0	0
South Africa	1916–74	0	0
Less-developed countries			
India	1958–63	4	1
	1973–76	n.a.	3
South Korea	1958–63	1	1
Marocco	1958–63	0	0
Phillipines	1958–63	8	0

Source: Greif [58, p. 733].

reason may be the operation of a deterrence effect. That is, given that compulsory licensing procedures are available, patent holders are more willing to negotiate licenses at arms length, without inviting the complexity and cost of a government compulsion action. However, this explanation is not very convincing, given the fact that in Canada and Great Britain, many formal pharmaceutical licensing actions have been brought despite the existence of clear, active pro-licensing policies.

In principle, compulsory licensing is appealing for two main reasons.

For one, the life of a patent and its strength are separate but interdependent policy variables. As a matter of general policy, uniform patent lives must be set. Any such decision entails errors on one side or the other. If one wishes to avoid the costs of fixing too short a patent life generally, one may set long lives and then deal with the relatively few special, high-cost cases individually, in effect reducing the patent's life or strength through a licensing action. This is not to say that the transaction costs incurred in a licensing action are small; quite clearly, they are not. Nor is it certain that government decision-makers' errors will not be more costly on balance that the costs imposed by leaving powerful patent positions in place. Few disagreements among economists are sharper than those weighing the social costs of the unfettered invisible hand against the costs of the intruding government hand.

A second advantage in principle of compulsory licensing is its ability to mitigate tendencies toward inefficient rent-seeking invention. Superior inventions would be available to all relevant users, dampening incentives to invent around rival patent positions. The general reduction in rent appropriation under "reasonable" royalty licensing discourages other forms of duplicative or excessively accelerated R&D investment.

The trouble with both of these arguments is the difficulty of finding the right compromise between too much and too little protection. A possible solution might be to institute a rebuttable legal presumption favoring compulsory licensing after some grace period has elapsed. If the patentee then comes foward to show that competition has not been lessened by the patent's force, or that unusual risks have been borne in conceiving or developing the invention, the licensing presumption would be waived. Again, such proceedings are neither costless nor error-free. How much social cost the policy itself would impose would depend upon how often patent holders petitioned for licensing waivers, which would depend upon the stringency of the burden of proof imposed upon petitioners. Since no such system exists at present, it is difficult to make confident predictions.

Especially in the United States, compulsory licensing has been used to open up markets to more competition when patents were instrumental in perpetuating monopoly power, cartelizing otherwise independent sellers, and excluding newcomers. In some 125 antitrust proceedings, tens of thousands of U.S. patents have been subjected to licensing, usually at "reasonable" royalty rates but sometimes royalty-free. Whole patent portfolios including thousands of patents have become accessible to competitors in certain cases. However, detailed analyses reveal that the goal of intensifying competition has been achieved only infrequently. Often, the antitrust decrees left the patent holders with many loopholes, such as the option to insist upon reciprocal licenses, which enabled them to retain their dominant positions [64, pp. 55–78]. On the more favorable side, the imposition of such large-scale compulsory licensing does not appear to have had seriously adverse R&D investment incentive effects. In a study of 42 U.S. companies subjected to compulsory licensing, Scherer [145, pp. 66–78] found that the targets did not have post-decree R&D/sales ratios lower than comparable counterpart firms not impacted by compulsory licensing. There was, however, some evidence that being subjected to compulsory licensing decrees reduced companies' propensity to patent and increased their propensity to keep inventions secret.

From the evidence available, it appears that compulsory licensing, if judiciously employed, could be used to open up dominant market positions to more competition without seriously reducing incentives to do research, invention, and development.

During the most active phase of previous century's anti-patent movement, economists tended to side with the anti-patent forces because of their commitment to free trade. After the movement collapsed, economists tended to leave patent questions largely to lawyers. Except in a few doctrinal questions, e.g., as to whether there is a "natural" property right in inventions, lawyers in turn were interested mostly in practical questions of patent system administration and adjudication. Research into historical questions was seldom deemed worth the effort. When the French patent law was enacted in 1791, for instance, the British patent system was hailed as the mother of British inventiveness and entrepreneurship, and the Statute of Monopolies was called the "Magna Charta" of all patent systems. See [155, pp. 1–5]. Patent system advocates focused repeatedly on the British law as the starting point of patent history. Even as literate an economist as Machlup wrote in 1964 [94] as if the patent system's chronicle spanned *only* three centuries.

We know now that another two centuries must be included, and we know that Venetian authorities during the 14th and 15th centuries learned by experience about most of the problems that lie at the core of today's patent economics analyses. To list but a few: To what extent should government foster technological change by financing contract research? Under what circumstances are prizes a suitable inducement to innovation? Under what conditions are patents superior? The Venetian government used all three approaches—contract research for naval weapons procurement, prizes for the construction of grain mills, and later patents for similar commercial ventures, especially during periods of financial stress.

The Venetian administration granted patents both with and without compulsory licensing provisions; it reserved a right for the government freely to use patented technologies for its own purposes; it repealed patents which were not utilized; and it granted patent lives varying between 5 and 80 years. All of these variants remain the subject of contemporary economic analyses of patent policy. Although a patent policy must be a compromise among diverse conflicting goals, and although the compromise struck today may for good reasons be quite different from those accepted five centuries ago, it is reassuring to learn that the economic problems of devising an optimal patent system have deep historical roots.

References

[1] Acs, Z. and D. B. Audretsch, "Innovation, Market Structure, and Firm Size," *Review of Economics and Statistics,* **69** (1987), 567–574.

[2] Adams, E. F., "The Legality of Compulsory Package Licensing of Patents," *Antitrust Bulletin,* **12** (1967), 773–804.

[3] Alderson, W., V. Terpstra, and S. J. Shapiro, eds., *Patents and Progress— The Sources and Impact of Advancing Technology.* Homewood, Ill.: Richard D. Irwin, 1965.

[4] Appelbaum, E. and E. Katz, "Seeking Rents by Setting Rents: The Political Economy of Rent Seeking," *Economic Journal,* **97** (1987), 685–699.

**[5] Arrow, K. J., "Economic Welfare and the Allocation of Resources for Invention," in *The Rate and Direction of Inventive Activity,* ed. by R. R. Nelson. New York: Princeton University Press, 1962.

[6] Arvidson, G., "A Note on Optimal Allocation of Resources for R&D," *The Swedish Journal of Economics,* **72** (1970), 171–195.

*[7] Baldwin, W. L. and J. T. Scott, *Market Structure and Technological Change,* vol. 17, Fundamentals of Pure and Applied Economics. Chur: Harwood Academic Publishers, 1987.

*[8] Balz, M., *Eigentumsordnung und Technologiepolitik.* Tübingen: J. C. B. Mohr (Paul Siebeck) Verlag, 1980.

[9] Baranson, J., *Technology and the Multinationals.* Lexington, Mass.: Lexington Books, D.C. Heath and Company, 1978.

[10] Barber, B., "Resistance by Scientists to Scientific Discovery, *Science* **134** (1961), 596–601.

*[11] Barzel, Y., "Optimal Timing of Innovations," *Review of Economics and Statistics,* **50** (1968), 248–355.

*[12] Beck, R. L., "Patents, Property Rights, and Social Welfare: Search for a Restricted Optimum," *Southern Economic Journal* **43** (1976), 1045–1055.

*[13] Beck, R. L., "Patents and Over-Investment in Process Inventions: Reply," *Southern Economic Journal,* 45 (1978), 289–292.

*[14] Beck, R. L., "Competition for Patent Monopolies," in *Research in Law and Economics,* ed. by R. O. Zerbe, **3** (1981), 91–100.

*[15] Beck, R. L., "The Prospect Theory of the Patent System and Unproductive Competition," *Research in Law and Economics,* **5** (1983), 193–209.

*[16] Beck, R. L., "Does Competitive Dissipation Require A Short Patent Life?", *Research in Law and Economics,* **8** (1987), 121–129.

**[17] Beer, J. J., "The Emergence of the German Dye Industry," *Illinois Studies in Social Sciences,* Vol. 44. Urbana, Ill.: University of Illinois Press, 1959.

[18] Berkowitz, M. K. and Y. Kotowitz, "Patent Policy in an Open Economy," *Canadian Journal of Economics,* **15** (1982), 1–17.

[19] Blackstone, E. A., "The Copying Machine Industry," Ph.D. dissertation, University of Michigan, 1968.

[20] Bond, R. S., and D. F. Lean, "Consumer Preference, Advertising and Sales; On the Advantage from Early Entry," Working Paper No. 14. Washington D.C.: U.S. Federal Trade Commission, Bureau of Economics, October 1979.

[21] Boston Consulting Group, *Perspectives on Experience.* Boston: Boston Consulting Group, 1972.

[22] Bowman, W. S., *Patent and Antitrust Law: A Legal and Economic Appraisal.* Chicago: University of Chicago Press, 1973.

[23] Bright, A. A., and W. R. Maclaurin, "Economic Factors Influencing the Development and Introduction of the Fluorescent Lamp," *Journal of Political Economy,* **51** (1943), 429–450.

[24] Bright, A. A., *The Electric Lamp Industry.* New York: Macmillan, 1949.

[25] Cave, J. A. K., "A Further Comment on Preemptive Patenting and the Persistence of Monopoly," *American Economic Review,* **75** (1985), 256–258.

[26] Caves, R. E., *Multinational Enterprise and Economic Analysis.* Cambridge: Cambridge University Press, 1982.

*[27] Caves, R. E., H. Crookell, and J. P. Killing, "The Imperfect Market for Technology Licenses," *Oxford Bulletin of Economics and Statistics,* **45** (1983), 249–267.

[28] Cheng, L., "International Trade and Technology: A Brief Survey," *Weltwirtschaftliches Archiv,* **120** (1984), 165–189.

[29] Cheung, S. N. S., "Property Rights in Trade Secrets," *Economic Inquiry,* **20** (1982), 40–53.

[30] Chevigny, P. G., "The Validity of Grant-Back Agreements under the Antitrust Laws," *Fordham Law Review,* **34** (1966), 569–592.

**[31] Cipolla, C. M., *Before the Industrial Revolution: European Society and Economy, 1000–1700.* London; Methuen & Co., 1976.

**[32] Conant, J. B., *Science and Common Sense.* New Haven: Yale University Press, 1951.

*[33] Conrad, C. A., "The Advantage of Being First and Competition between Firms," *International Journal of Industrial Organization,* **1** (1983), 353–364.

*[34] Contractor, F. J., *International Technology Licensing: Compensation,*

Costs, and Negotiation. Lexington, Mass.: Lexington Books, D. C. Heath and Company, 1981.

[35] Corry, C. S., *Compulsory Licensing of Patents—A Legislative History*, Study No. 12 of the Senate Subcommittee on Patents, Trademarks, and Copyrights. Washington, D.C.: Government Printing Office, 1958.

[36] Crotti, A. E., "The German Gebrauchsmuster", *Journal of the Patent Office Society*, **39** (1957), 566–582.

[37] Dasgupta, P. S., and J. E. Stiglitz, "Industrial Structure and the Nature of Inventive Activity," *Economic Journal*, **90** (1986), 266–293.

[38] DeBrock, L. M., "Market Structure, Innovation, and Optimal Patent Life," *Journal of Law and Economics*, **28** (1985), 223–244.

[39] Demsetz, H., "Toward a Theory of Property Rights," *American Economic Review*, Papers and Proceedings, **57** (1967), 347–359.

[40] Dietz, A., *Das Patentrecht der südosteuropäischen Staaten.* Weinheim; Verlag Chemie, 1983.

[41] Enos, J. L., *Petroleum Progress and Profits.* Cambridge, Mass.: MIT Press, 1962.

[42] Evenson, R. E., "International Invention: Implications for Technology Market Analysis," in *R&D, Patents, and Productivity*, ed. by Z. Griliches. Chicago: University of Chicago Press, 1984.

[43] Faust, K., and H. Schedl, *Internationale Wettbewerbsfähigkeit und struktruelle Anpassungserfordernisse.* Ifo-Studien zur Strukturforschung, Vol. 3, Munich, Ifo-Institut, 1984.

[44] Federal Trade Commission, *Report to the Federal Trade Commission on Federal Energy Land Policy.* U.S. Senate Committee on Interior and Insular Affairs. Washington, D.C.: Government Printing Office, 1976.

[45] Federico, P. J., *Distribution on Patents Issued to Corporations, 1939–1955.* Study No. 3 of the Senate Subcommittee on Patents, Trademarks, and Copyrights. Washington, D.C.: Government Printing Office, 1958.

[46] Federico, P. J., *Renewal Fees and Other Patent Fees in Foreign Countries*, Study No. 17 of the Senate Subcommittee on Patents, Trademarks, and Copyrights. Washington, D.C.: Government Printing Office, 1958.

[47] Freeman, Christopher, *Industrial Innovation.* London; Harmondsworth: Penguin, 1974.

[48] Geroski, P. A., and A. Jacquemin, "Dominant Firms and Their Alleged Decline," *International Journal of Industrial Organization*, **2** (1984), 1–27.

[49] Gilbert, R. J., and D. M. G. Newberry, "Preemptive Patenting and the Persistence of Monopoly," *American Economic Review*, **72** (1982), 514–526.

[50] Gilbert, R. J., "Uncertain Innovation and the Persistence of Monopoly: Comment," *American Economic Review*, **74** (1984), 238–242.

[51] Gilbert, R. J., "Preemptive Patenting and the Persistence of Monopoly: Reply," *American Economic Review*, **74** (1984), 251–253.

[52] Gilfillan, S. C., *Invention and the Patent System* (Materials Relating to Continuing Studies of Technology, Economic Growth, and the Variability of Private Investment), Joint Economic Committee, Congress of the United States). Washington, D.C.: Government Printing Office, 1964.

*[53] Glazer, A., "The Advantage of Being First," *American Economic Review*, **75** (1985), 473–480.

[54] Gorecki, P. K., *Regulating the Price of Prescription Drugs in Canada*: *Compulsory Licensing, Product Selection, and Government Reimbursement*

Programs. Economic Council of Canada, Technical Report No. 8. Ottawa, Ontario, May, 1981.

*[55] Greer, D., "The Case Against the Patent System in Less-Developed Countries," *Journal of International Law and Economics,* **8** (1973), 223–226.

[56] Grefermann, K., K. H. Oppenländer, E. Peffgen, K. Ch. Röthlingshöfer, and L. Scholz, *Patentwesen und technischer Fortschritt.* Teil I: Die Wirkung des Patentwesens im Innovationsprozess. Göttingen: Verlag Otto Schwarz & Co, 1974.

[57] Greif, S., "Zur voraussichtlichen Inanspruchnahme des Europa-Patents durch deutsche Anmelder," *Gewerblicher Rechtsschutz und Urheberrecht, Internationaler Teil,* Heft **11 (1977), 379–393.

[58] Greif, S., "Ausübungszwang für Patente," *Gewerblicher Rechtsschutz und Urheberrecht,* Internationaler Teil, Heft **12** (1981), 731–745.

[59] Greif, S., *Angebot und Nachfrage nach Patent information-Die Informationsfunktion von Patenten.* Göttingen: Verlag Otto Schwarz & Co, 1982.

**[60] Greipel, E., and U. Taeger, *Auswirkungen des Patentschutzes und der Lizenzvergabepraxis auf den Wettbewerb in ausgewählten Wirtschaftsbereichen unter besonderer Berücksichtigung der Marktsituation kleiner und mittlerer Unternehmen,* Gutachten erstellt für das Bundeswirtschaftsministerium in Bonn. Munich: Ifo-Institut, May 1981.

[61] Griliches, Z., "Research Expenditures, Education, and the Aggregate Agricultural Production Function," *American Economic Review,* 54 (1964), 961–974.

*[62] Hart, P. E., "Experience Curves and Industrial Policy," *International Journal of Industrial Organization,* 1 (1983), 95–106.

[63] Hiance, M., and Y. Plasseraraud, *Brevets et Sous-Developpment: La Protection des Inventions dans la Tiers-Monde.* Paris: Librairies Techniques, 1972.

*[64] Hollabaugh, M. A., and R. Wright, *Compulsory Licensing under Antitrust Judgements,* Staff Report, Senate Subcommittee on Patents, Trademarks, and Copyrights. Washington, D.C.: Government Printing Office, 1960.

[65] Isay, H., *Die Funktion der Patente im Wirtschaftskampf.* Berlin: Franz Vahlen Verlag, 1927.

[66] Jewkes, J., D. Sawers, and R. Stillerman. *The Sources of Invention.* London: Macmillan, 1962.

[67] Johnson, H. G., "Aspects of Patents and Licenses as Stimuli to Innovation," *Weltwirtschaftliches Archiv,* **112** (1976), 417–428.

*[68] Kahn, A. E., "The Role of Patents," in *Competition, Cartels and Their Regulation,* ed. by J. P. Miller, Amsterdam: North-Holland Publishing Company, 1962.

*[69] Kamien, M. I., and N. L. Schwartz, "Patent Life and R&D Rivalry," *American Economic Review,* 64 (1974), 183–187.

*[70] Kamien, M. I., and N. L. Schwartz, *Market Structure and Innovation.* Cambridge: Cambridge University Press, 1982.

[71] Katz, M. L., and C. Shapiro, "R&D Rivalry with Licensing or Imitation," *American Economic Review,* **77** (1987), 402–420.

*[72] Kaysen, C., *United States vs. United Shoe Machinery Corporation.* Cambridge, Mass.: Harvard University Press, 1956.

[73] Keller, P., "Hundert Jahre Internationaler Patentschutz: Aufbau und Entwicklung eines Vöker rechtsinstruments," *Neue Zürcher Zeitung,* March 22, 1983, p. 15.

[74] Kitch, E. W., "Graham vs. John Deere Co.: New Standards for Invention," *The Supreme Court Review,* 1966, 293–346.

[75] Kitch, E. W., "The Nature and Function of the Patent System," *Journal of Law and Economics,* **20** (1977), 265–290.

[76] Kitch, E. W., "Patents, Prospects, and Economic Surplus: A Reply," *Journal of Law and Economics,* **23** (1980), 205–207.

[77] Kitti, C., "Patent Policy and the Optimal Timing of Innovations," Ph.D. dissertation, University of Chicago, 1973.

[78] Klein, B. H., "A Radical Proposal for R&D," *Fortune,* May 1958, 112–113, 218–226.

[79] Krueger, A. O., "The Political Economy of the Rent Seeking Society," *American Economic Review,* **64** (1974), 291–303.

[80] Landau, D. L., "Patents and Over-Investment in Process Inventions? Comment," *Southern Economic Journal,* 45 (1978), 285–288.

[81] Landes, D. S., *Revolution in Time: Clocks and the Making of the Modern World.* Cambridge, Mass.; Belknap Press of Harvard University Press, 1983.

[82] Landesarchiv Innsbruck, Pestarchiv, XIV Repertorium 42 E IX Nr. 603: Erfynndung und Perkhwerks Ordnung der Loeblichen Graueschaft Tirol, 1408 (Schladminger Bergbrief).

[83] Landesarchiv Innsbruck, Pestarchiv, XIV Repertorium 42 E IX Nr. 648: Statuto Mineraria, 1488, deutsche Fassung.

[84] Leontief, W., "On Assignment of Patent Rights on Inventions Made under Government Research Contracts," *Harvard Law Review,* **77** (1964), 492–497.

[85] Letwin, W., "The English Common Law Concerning Monopolies," *University of Chicago Law Review,* **21** (1954), 355–385.

[86] Levin, R. C., "Technical Change, Barriers to Entry and Market Structure," *Economica,* 45 (1978), 347–362.

[87] Levin, R. C., A. K. Klevorick, R. R. Nelson, and S. G. Winter, "Appropriating the Returns from Industrial R&D," *Brookings Papers on Economic Activity* (1988).

[88] Levin, R. C., W. M. Cohen, and D. C. Mowery, "R&D Appropriability, Opportunity, and Market Structure: New Evidence on Some Schumpeterian Hypotheses," *American Economic Review,* Papers and Proceedings, **75** (1985), 20–24.

[89] Loury, G., "Market Structure and Innovation," *Quarterly Journal of Economics,* 93 (1979), 395–409.

[90] Lutz, M. J., "China auf dem Weg zu einer Patent- und Markenpraxis—Ein Symposium in Peking," *Neue Zürcher Zeitung,* 206 (1985), No. 272, 14.

[91] Machlup, F., and E. T. Penrose, "The Patent Controversy in the Nineteenth Century," *Journal of Economic History,* **10** (1950), 1–29.

[92] Machlup, F., *An Economic Review of the Patent System,* Study No. 15 of the Senate Subcommittee on Patents, Trademarks, and Copyrights. Washington, D.C.: Government Printing Office, 1958.

[93] Machlup, F., "The Optimum Lag of Imitation Behind Innovation," *Nationalokonomisk Tidsskrift,* Festskrift til Frederic Zeuthen, **96** (1958), 239–256.

[94] Machlup, F., "Patentwesen: Geschichtlicher Übcrblick," *Handwörterbuch der Sozialwissenschaften,* **8** (1964), 231–240. Stuttgart: Gustav Fischer Verlag, 1964.

[95] Maclaurin, W. R., "Patents and Technical Progress: A Study of Television," *Journal of Political Economy,* **58** (1950), 142–157.

[96] Maclaurin, W. R., "Technological Progress in Some American Industries," *American Economic Review,* Papers and Proceedings, **44 (1954), 178–189.

[97] Mandich, G., "Privative Industriali Veneziani (1450–1550)," *Rivista di Diritto Commerciale,* **1 (1936), 511–547.

[98] Mandich, G., "Primi Riconoscimenti Veneziani di un Diritto di Privativi agli Inventori," *Rivista di Diritto Industriale,* **1 (1958), 101–155.

[99] Mansfield, E., "Rates of Return from Industrial Development," *American Economic Review,* Papers and Proceedings, **55** (1965), 310–322.

*[100] Mansfield, E., J. Rapoport, A. Romeo, S. Wagner, and G. Beardsley, "Social and Private Rates of Return from Industrial Innovations," *Quarterly Journal of Economics,* **71** (1977), 221–240.

*[101] Mansfield, E., M. Schwartz, and S. Wagner, "Imitation Costs and Patents: An Empirical Study," *Economic Journal,* **91** (1981), 907–918.

[102] Markham, J. W., "The Joint Effect of Antitrust and Patent Laws upon Innovation," *American Economic Review,* Papers and Proceedings, **56** (1966), 291–300.

[103] Marschak, T. A., "The Role of Project Histories in the Study of Research and Development," RAND Corporation Study No. P-2850. Santa Monica, Cal., 1965.

[104] McFetridge, D. G., *Government Support of Scientific Research and Development: An Economic Analysis.* Toronto: University of Toronto Press, 1977.

[105] McFetridge, D. G., and D. A. Smith, "Patents, Prospects, and Economic Surplus:: A Comment," *Journal of Law and Economics,* **23** (1980), 197–203.

*[106] McFetridge, D. G., and M. Rafiquzzaman, "The Scope and Duration of the Patent Right and the Nature of Research Rivalry," *Research in Law and Economics,* **8** (1986), 91–120.

*[107] McGee, J. S., "Patent Exploitation: Some Economic and Legal Problems," *Journal of Law and Economics,* **9** (1966), 135–162.

[108] Melman, S., *The Impact of the Patent System on Research,* Study No. 11 of the Senate Subcommittee on Patents, Trademarks, and Copyrights. Washington; Government Printing Office, 1958.

*[109] Mestmäcker, E. J., *Europäisches Wettbewerbsrecht.* Munich: C. H. Beck Verlag, 1974.

[110] Minasian, J. R., "The Economics of Research and Development," in R. R. Nelson, ed., *The Rate and Direction of Inventive Activity,* pp. 93–141. Princeton: Princeton University Press, 1962.

[111] Moellering, K. T., "Die Alterserwartung deutscher Patente," *Zeitschrift für die gesamte Staatswissenschaft,* **106 (1950) 719–749.

[112] Needham, D., "The Incentive Theory of Patent Protection," Ph.D. dissertation, Princeton University, 1965.

[113] Nelson, R. R., and S. G. Winter, *An Evolutionary Theory of Economic Change.* Cambridge, Mass.: Belknap Press of Harvard University Press, 1982.

**[114] Neumeyer, F., "Die historischen Grundlagen der ersten modernen Patentgesetze in den USA und in Frankreich," *Gewerblicher Rechtschutz und Urheberrecht*, Internationaler Tiel, (1956), 241–252.

*[115] Neumeyer, F., *Compulsory Licensing of Patents under Some Non-American Systems*, Study No. 19 of the Senate Subcommittee on Patents, Trademarks, and Copyrights. Washington, D.C: Government Printing Office, 1959.

[116] Neumeyer, F., "Patent und Beschränkung des Wettbewerbs," *Wirtschaft und Recht*, **12** (1969), 240–251.

[117] Nordhaus, R. C., and E. F. Jurow, *Patent-Antitrust Law*. Chicago: Jural Publishing Co., 1961.

[118] Nordhaus, R. C., *Patent License Agreements*. Chicago: Jural Publishing Co., 1967.

*[119] Nordhaus, W. D., "The Optimal Life of a Patent," Cowles Foundation Discussion Paper No. 241. New Haven: Cowles Foundation for Research in Economics, 1967.

*[120] Nordhaus, W. D., *Invention, Growth, and Welfare: A Theoretical Treatment of Technological Change*. Cambridge, Mass.: MIT Press, 1969.

*[121] Öhlschlegel, H., *Das Bergrecht als Ursprung des Patentrechts*, Technikgeschichte in Einzeldarstellungen, Nr. 30, Düsseldorf: VDI Verlag, 1978.

[122] Oppenländer, K. H., ed, *Patentwesen, technischer Fortschritt und Wettbewerb*. Göttingen: Verlag Otto Schwartz, 1974.

*[123] Pakes, A., and M. Schankerman, "The Rate of Obsolescence of Patents, Research Gestation Lags, and the Private Rate of Return to Research Resources," in *R&D, Patents, and Productivity*, ed. Z. Griliches. Chicago: University of Chicago Press, 1984.

[124] Peck, M. J., and F. M. Scherer, *The Weapons Acquisition Process: An Economic Analysis*. Boston: Harvard Business School Division of Research, 1962.

*[125] Penrose, E. T., *The Economics of the International Patent System*. Baltimore: Johns Hopkins University Press, 1951.

*[126] Penrose, E., "International Patenting and the Less-Developed Countries," *Economic Journal*, **83** (1973), 768–786.

[127] Plant, A., "The Economic Theory Concerning Patents for Inventions," *Economica*, New Series, 1 (1934), 30–51.

[128] Posner, R. A., "The Social Costs of Monopoly and Regulation," *Journal of Political Economy*, **83** (1975), 807–827.

[129] Pribam, K., *Geschichte der Österreichischen Gewerbepolitik von 1740–1860*, vol. 1. Leipzig: Duncker und Humblot, 1907.

*[130] Priest, G. L., "Cartels and Patent License Agreements," *Journal of Law and Economics*, **20** (1977), 309–378.

*[131] Reinganum, J. F., "Uncertain Innovation and the Persistence of Monopoly," *American Economic Review*, **73** (1983), 741–748.

*[132] Salant, S. W., "Preemptive Patenting and the Persistence of Monopoly: Comment," *American Economic Review*, **74** (1984), 247–250.

[133] Sanders, B. S., J. Rossman, and L. J. Harris, "The Economic Impact of Patents," *Patent, Trademark, and Copyright Journal of Research and Education*, **2** (1958), 340–362.

[134] Sanders, B. S., "Speedy Entry of Patented Inventions into Commercial Use," *Patent Trademark, and Copyright Journal of Research and Education*, **6** (1962), 87–116.

[135] Sanders, B. S., "Patterns of Commercial Exploitation of Patented Inventions by Large and Small Corporations," *Patent, Trademark, and Copyright Journal of Research and Education,* **8** (1964), 51–93.

[136] Sandor, R. L., "Some Empirical Findings on the Legal Costs of Patenting," *Journal of Business,* **45** (1972), 375–378.

*[137] Scherer, F. M., ed., *Patents and the Corporation*: *A Report on Industrial Technology under Changing Public Policy.* Boston: J. J. Galvin, 1958.

[138] Scherer, F. M., *The Weapons Acquisition Process*: *Economic Incentives.* Boston: Harvard Business School Division of Research, 1964.

*[139] Scherer, F. M., "Invention and Innovation in the Watt-Boulton Steam-Engine Venture," *Technology and Culture,* **6** (1965), 165–187.

*[140] Scherer, F. M., "Firm Size, Market Structure, Opportunity, and the Output of Patented Inventions," *American Economic Review,* **55** (1965), 1097–1125.

*[141] Scherer, F. M., "Time-Cost Tradeoffs in Uncertain Empirical Research Projects," *Naval Research Logistics Quarterly,* **13** (1966), 71–82.

*[142] Scherer, F. M., "Research and Development Resource Allocation under Rivalry," *Quarterly Journal of Economics,* **81** (1967), 359–394.

*[143] Scherer, F. M., "Market Structure and the Employment of Scientists and Engineers," *American Economic Review,* **57** (1967), 524–531.

*[144] Scherer, F. M., "Nordhaus' Theory of Optimal Patent Life: A Geometric Reinterpretation," *American Economic Review,* **62** (1972), 422–427.

*[145] Scherer, F. M., *The Economic Effects of Compulsory Patent Licensing,* Monograph Series in Finance and Economics, 1977–2. New York: New York University, 1977.

*[146] Scherer, F. M., "The Welfare Economics of Product Variety: An Application to the Ready-to-Eat Cereals Industry," *Journal of Industrial Economics,* **28** (1979), 113–134.

*[147] Scherer, F. M., *Industrial Market Structure and Economic Performance,* 2nd ed. Boston: Houghton-Mifflin, 1980.

*[148] Scherer, F. M., "The Propensity to Patent," *International Journal of Industrial Organization,* **1** (1983), 107–128.

**[149] Scherer, F. M., "The World Productivity Growth Slump," in *Organizing Industrial Development,* ed. Rolf Wolff, pp. 15–27. Berlin; Walter de Gruyter, 1986.

*[150] Schiff, E., *Industrialization without Patents.* Princeton: Princeton University Press, 1971.

*[151] Schmalensee, R., "Product Differentiation Advantages of Pioneering Brands," *American Economic Review,* **72** (1982), 349–365.

*[152] Schmookler, J., *Invention and Economic Growth.* Cambridge, Mass.; Harvard University Press, 1966.

*[153] Schmookler, J., *Patents, Invention, and Economic Change.* Cambridge, Mass.: Harvard University Press, 1972.

[154] Shapiro, C., "Patent Licensing and R&D Rivalry," *American Economic Review,* Papers and Proceedings, **75** (1985), 25–30.

*[155] Silberstein, M., *Erfindungsschutz und merkantilistische Handelsprivilegien.* Winterthur: Verlag P.G. Keller, 1961.

[156] Silberston, A., "The Patent System," *Lloyds Bank Review,* No. 84 (1967), 32–44.

*[157] Spence, A. M., "Product Selection, Fixed Costs, and Monopolistic Competition," *Review of Economic Studies,* **43** (1976), 217–235.

[158] Spence, A. M., "The Learning Curve and Competition," *Bell Journal of Economics*, 12 (1981), 49–70.
[159] Stillerman, R., "Resistance to Change," *Journal of the Patent Office Society*, 48 (1966), 484–499.
[160] Stocking, G. W., and M. W. Watkins, *Cartels in Action*. New York: Twentieth Century Fund, 1949.
[161] Sturmey, S. G., *The Economic Development of Radio*. London: Gerald Duckworth & Co., 1958.
[162] Taeger, U. C., *Untersuchung der Aussagefähigkeit von Patentstatistiken hinsichtlich technologischer Entwicklungen*. Ifo-Studien zur Industriewirtschaft, Vol. 17, Munich: Ifo-Institut, 1979.
*[163] Tandon, P., "Optimal Patents with Compulsory Licensing," *Journal of Political Economy*, 90 (1982), 470–486.
*[164] Taylor, C. T., and Z. A. Silberston, *The Economic Impact of the Patent System: A Study of the British Experience*. Cambridge: Cambridge University Press, 1973.
ᵗ*[165] Teece, D. J., "Technology Transfer by Multinational Firms: The Resource Cost of Transfering Technological Know-how," *Economic Journal*, 87 (1977), 241–261.
[166] Teece, D. J., *The Multinational Corporation and the Resource Cost of International Technology Transfer*. Cambridge, Mass.: Ballinger, 1977.
*[167] Telesio, P., *Technology Licensing and Multinational Enterprises*. New York: Praeger, 1979.
[168] Tullock, G., "The Welfare Costs of Tariffs, Monopolies, and Theft," *Western Economic Journal*, 5 (1967), 224–232.
*[169] Turner, D. F., "The Patent System and Competitive Policy," *New York University Law Review*, 44 (1969), 450–476.
*[170] UNCTAD, *The Role of the Patent System in the Transfer of Technology to Developing Countries*. New York: United Nations, 1975.
*[171] UNCTAD, *The International Patent System: The Revision of the Paris Convention for Protection of Industrial Property*. New York: United Nations, 1977.
*[172] Usher, A. P., *A History of Mechanical Inventions*, rev. ed. Cambridge, Mass.: Harvard University Press, 1954.
*[173] Usher, D., "The Welfare Economics of Invention," *Economica*, 31 (1964), 279–287.
*[174] Vaughan, F. L., *The United States Patent System: Legal and Economic Conflicts in American Patent History*. Norman: University of Oklahoma Press, 1956.
**[175] von Gehr, G., "A Survey of the Principal National Patent Systems," *John Marshall Law Quarterly*, 1 (1936), 110–158, 334–400.
*[176] von Weizsäcker, C. C., *Barriers to Entry: A Theoretical Treatment*. Heidelberg: Springer Verlag, 1980.
[177] von Weizsäcker, C. C., "Rechte und Verhältnisse in der modernen Wirtschaftslehre," *Kyklos*, 34 (1981), 345–376.
*[178] Wagner, A., *Grundlegung der politischen Oekonomie*, Zweiter Theil: Volkswirtschaft und Recht, besonders Vermögensrecht oder Freiheit und Eigenthum in volkswirtschaftlicher Betrachtung. Leipzig; C. F. Winter'sche Verlagshandlung, 1894.
**[179] Whitehead, A. N., *Wissenschaft und moderne Welt*. Zürich: Morgaten Verlag, 1949; *Science and Modern World*, New York: Macmillan 1925.

[180] Wilson, R. W., "The Effect of Technology Environment and Product Rivalry on R&D Effort and Licensing of Inventions," *Review of Economics and Statistics,* **59** (1977), 171–178.

[181] Winkler, G., "Das neue Gebrauchsmustergesetz," *Mitteilungen der deutschen Patentanwälte,* **78** (1987), 3–8.

*[182] Wright, B. D., "The Economics of Invention Incentives: Patents, Prizes, and Research Contracts," *American Economic Review,* **73** (1983), 691–707.

*[183] Yu, B. T., "Potential Competition and Contracting in Innovation," *Journal of Law and Economics,* **24** (1981), 215–238.

[184] Zycha, A., *Das böhmische Bergrecht des Mittelalters auf der Grundlage des Bergrechts von Iglau,* vol. 2. Berlin: Verlag Franz Vahlen, 1900.

INDEX

For Product Safety Concerns and Information please contact our EU
representative GPSR@taylorandfrancis.com Taylor & Francis Verlag GmbH,
Kaufingerstraße 24, 80331 München, Germany

Printed and bound by CPI Group (UK) Ltd, Croydon, CR0 4YY

12/05/2025

01867573-0001